27

# Annabel **Karmel's**
# New Baby and Toddler Cookbook

*To Nicholas, Lara and Scarlett and all the other children who tasted the recipes for this book – happy and healthy eating for life*

# Annabel**Karmel's**
# New Baby and Toddler Cookbook

## More tempting, nutritious and easy-to-cook recipes for young children

EBURY PRESS
LONDON

7 9 10 8 6

First published in the United Kingdom in 1995 by Ebury Press

This revised edition published in 2000 by Ebury Press
Random House · 20 Vauxhall Bridge Road · London SW1V 2SA

Random House Australia (Pty) Limited
20 Alfred Street, Milsons Point · Sydney · New South Wales 2061 · Australia

Random House New Zealand Limited
18 Poland Road · Glenfield · Auckland 10 · New Zealand

Random House South Africa (Pty) Limited
Endulini · 5a Jubilee Road · Parktown 2193 · South Africa

Random House Canada
1265 Aerowood Drive · Mississauga · Ontario L4W 1B9

Random House Group Limited Reg No. 954009

www.randomhouse.co.uk

A CIP catalogue for this book is available from the British Library

0 09 182558 X

Designed by Lovelock & Co. · Illustrations by Susan Hellard

Colour reproduction by Colorlito, Milan

Printed and bound in China by Midas Printing Ltd.

Papers used by Ebury Press are natural recyclable products made from wood grown in sustainable forests.

# Contents

# Introduction

Losing my first child, Natasha, a perfectly healthy baby, to a viral infection at the tender age of eleven weeks, made me painfully aware of the vulnerability of young children. She died in my arms at Great Ormond Street Hospital five days after she was admitted, and I felt devastated that there was absolutely nothing I could do to help her.

After Natasha's death, I wanted to channel my grief into something positive that would help other mothers, so I began to look into the whole subject of feeding babies and young children. In early childhood, eating habits and tastes are formed for life. A bad diet is one of the main causes of illness and premature death in adults in developed countries. A well-stocked larder is the best form of preventive medicine known to man. Three years later saw the publication of my first book, *The Complete Baby and Toddler Meal Planner*, which I am happy to say has introduced babies all over the world to the pleasures of English nursery food and home cooking.

My son Nicholas was born one year after Natasha's death, and made a rather sudden and dramatic appearance at the top of our staircase into the trembling arms of my husband Simon. Nicholas's initial impatience to see the world was reflected in his eating habits. Life was far too exciting to spend time eating when there was so much to explore, and there were really only three foods that he enjoyed – fruit, pasta and ice-cream. Everything else was met with a stubbornness that belied his tender age. Being such a food lover myself, I couldn't believe that my young son wouldn't be like me, and mealtimes turned into a battle of wills, to be endured rather than enjoyed. Nearly every baby goes through a phase of fussy eating, picking at food before pushing the plate away, or flatly refusing to eat at mealtimes. The trouble often begins around the age of one year and very often the more children are entreated to eat, the less likely they are to comply. A good deal of psychology is required in feeding babies and toddlers, and certain ingredients may need an element of disguise. The section 'When Baby Says No!' gives lots of practical advice and handy tips on how to cope with fussy and problem eaters.

Nicholas, now eleven and a good healthy eater, was my first guinea pig, then along came Lara, now ten, who loved anything red out of a can or bottle, and Scarlett, seven, who wanted to start and finish her meal with ice-cream. I had three different ages and stages on which to try out and test my experiments in the kitchen, not to mention the big baby in the family, my husband Simon, who stoically ate his way through all the following recipes!

This book acts as a concise guide to a healthy diet, looking at ways in which to improve your child's health, performance and behaviour by choosing the right foods. Then there is a multitude of easy-to-prepare, mouth-watering recipes from finger foods to family meals, taking you from the first recipes for purées when weaning your baby off an all-milk diet, through to healthy meat, fish, pasta and fruit dishes, and snacks and teatime treats that will delight both adults and children of all ages.

All these recipes – and there are over 150 brand-new ones! – should give you plenty to choose from, because it's all too easy to get stuck in a rut and serve up the same old meals day after day. For we should be trying to broaden the range of foods that our children can enjoy, since children generally make up their minds by the age of five which foods they will eat and which they won't touch. Often our attempts at home cooking take second place to sausages and chips, and it's easier to give in to our 'junk-food junkies' than to be faced with a fraught emotional battle and the dreaded words that cut close to any parent's heart, 'That's yucky, I'm not eating it!'

Children in general are eating more junk food now than ever before, but it's only while they are young that we parents have control over what our children eat. Children have no preconceived ideas about food unless they get used to the ever-present sausages, chips and chicken nuggets. I know that many children given half a chance would live on burgers, pizzas, chips and ice lollies. However, junk foods are generally high in calories but low in nutrients and underneath the salt, monosodium glutamate, the tasty orange breadcrumbs and batters often lurk inferior products like reconstituted fish or fatty minced meat. As a result I've concocted some really appealing 'Healthy Fast Food' recipes for children's perennial favourites, and a guide to healthier snacks as well.

'Larder Layabouts' looks at the best foods to store in your larder and shows how easy it is to conjure up delicious meals from the contents of your store cupboard on the spur of the moment. There are also new ways of presenting favourite foods with fresh ingredients like my fish finger kebabs, to give them guaranteed child appeal.

Every one of the recipes has been given a seal of approval, having been tested on panels of children who had to give it the 'thumbs-up' before it could be included in this book. I have tried to achieve a balance between the foods which I think children will like and those which also exhibit good nutritional values. In this regard, I have been invaluably aided by and I am greatly indebted to Margaret Lawson, senior lecturer in Paediatric Nutrition at Great Ormond Street Hospital for Sick Children.

The 'proof of the pudding is in the eating', so go on – have a go. It's fun, it's healthy and it will give you a lot of personal satisfaction knowing that you are doing something worth-while for your children which will set them up for a healthy life.

# CHAPTER ONE

# Food for Thought

Growing children need plenty of energy, and a healthy appetite will usually make sure that they get enough calories from their food, but it's easy to get into the habit of eating the *wrong* foods. Sausages, chips, pizzas, chocolate and ice-cream are all very appealing, but if your child eats too much fat and sugar he may miss out on the nutrients that matter and lay down the foundations of heart disease and other health problems in later life. It is much better to give these kinds of foods only very occasionally rather than allowing them to become an important part of your child's diet.

Young children don't understand the importance of good nutrition so it is up to us as parents to set them a healthy eating pattern for the rest of their lives. The pre-school years are the only time we have almost complete control over our children's diets. You control what your child eats, and she controls how much.

Young children are at the stage of developing taste, so it is important to try to train them to enjoy foods that are naturally sweet rather than let them acquire a taste for sugar-loaded foods. Do not buy or offer sugary cereals, cakes and tinned fruits. Foods should be flavoured with herbs or just *lightly* salted.

As children become more independent and make their own choices, you can encourage them in the right direction by having a good supply of the right foods available. But what are the right foods to give our children? In the next few pages, you will learn about the foods that are important for your child so try to make them a regular part of her diet. It's a good time to review your own diet too, and it helps to set a good example as young children particularly are influenced by what they see their parents eating.

## GUIDELINES FOR A HEALTHY DIET

Choosing a balanced diet is a matter of eating foods in the right proportion, and the purpose of the food guide pyramid is to help you think in terms of food *groups* rather than individual foods. Your body needs more of some foods and less of others. If the food comes from the bottom of the pyramid, add more of it to your diet and eat less from the food groups nearer the top of the pyramid. In other words, eat plenty of grains, vegetables and fruits, a moderate amount from the meat and milk groups, and limit fatty and sweet foods as much as possible.

The pyramid diet is suitable for children of three years and over, although you should aim towards this from the start. The big difference with younger children, particularly in the first year, is that the diet is heavily weighted towards milk. Also, babies and toddlers need more fat and less fibre than adults because fat is an important source of energy. Weaning diets that are too low in energy may affect a baby's growth and development. Similarly, babies should not be given a lot of fibre as too much can fill a baby's stomach before enough calories are consumed.

It is hard to know how much food children need to grow normally, as each individual has his or her own requirements. Some children eat as much as adults, and other children seem to thrive on very small amounts of food. As a parent it can be very worrying to have a child who shows little interest in food, but you can take comfort in the knowledge that it is very common for young children to eat very little – a child who is healthy and has plenty of energy is probably getting all the food he or she needs.

- Eat plenty of fresh fruit and vegetables, keep a well-stocked fruit bowl, and have plenty of salad or crisp vegetables for your child to nibble on.
- Avoid eating too much saturated fat.
- Don't eat sugary foods too often, particularly between meals.
- Don't eat too much salt and don't add salt before one year.
- Eat plenty of foods rich in iron.
- Eat a good variety of foods.

Produced by the Flour Advisory Bureau and the Dunn Nutrition Centre

- Avoid processed foods, and read labels carefully (see also Misleading Labelling, page 162).
- Grill, microwave, steam or bake rather than fry foods.
- Avoid refined products like white bread, sugar-coated breakfast cereals, biscuits and cakes.
- Choose some food from each of the main four food groups – dairy products, starchy foods, vegetables and fruit, meat and meat alternatives – every day, and try to eat food from at least two of these groups at each meal.

It is the overall balance of the diet that is important, so look at your child's diet over the period of a week rather than worrying about balancing each individual meal. Don't drive yourself crazy if your child prefers Rice Krispies to porridge, just be glad he's getting the milk in his cereal!

## STARCHY FOODS
***Main nutrients provided:* starch, fibre, B vitamins, protein, energy and minerals**

| | |
|---|---|
| Bread | Potatoes |
| Breakfast cereals | Sweet potatoes |
| Pasta | Sweetcorn |
| Rice | Plantains (green bananas) |

- Before six months, give low-fibre, rice-based cereal (this avoids possible allergic reactions); work towards wholegrain by the age of one year.
- Buy and offer wholegrain products like wholemeal bread, brown rice, wholemeal flour, wheatgerm and wholegrain breakfast cereals like porridge or muesli. They contain more vitamins and minerals and are rich in fibre which helps to prevent constipation. Try to keep a good range of interesting breads and healthy biscuits in your larder.
- Starchy foods give us energy. They're usually cheap and are not high in calories unless we add fat or sugar.

- Don't add extra fibre like wheat bran as it can interfere with your child's absorption of minerals, particularly calcium, zinc and iron. Be careful not to give too many high-fibre foods as your child may feel full before getting sufficient nutrients and energy.

## VEGETABLES AND FRUITS

*Main nutrients provided*: **vitamins, minerals, fibre and sugars**

### VEGETABLES AND FRUITS RICH IN VITAMIN C

Brussels sprouts
Green peppers
Cauliflower
Broccoli
Cabbage
Peas

Citrus fruits
Berry fruits
Blackcurrants
Guava
Strawberries
Kiwi

### VEGETABLES AND FRUITS RICH IN VITAMIN A

Carrots
Broccoli
Dark green leafy vegetables
Sweet potato
Tomatoes

Plums
Apricots, dried and fresh
Cantaloupe melon
Mango
Papaya
Peach

- Try to include a total of five helpings from this group daily.
- To preserve vitamins, try to encourage your children to eat as many raw fruits and vegetables as possible. Raw vegetables served with a dip and skewers of fresh fruit are very popular with children.

- Most of the vitamins in fruit and vegetables lie just beneath the skin. Wash fruits and vegetables carefully and leave the skin on whenever possible.
- The best method of cooking vegetables to retain maximum nutrients is to steam, stir-fry or microwave them. Broccoli, steamed or microwaved, retains over 80 per cent of its Vitamin C whereas boiled broccoli retains only about 30 per cent. Vitamins C and B are water-soluble and are lost in the cooking water if vegetables are boiled. If you do need to boil vegetables, use the minimum amount of water, cook them for as short a time as possible and if you are making a sauce, try and use the cooking liquid in it. However, in order to ensure your child receives the maximum benefit from vegetables encourage him to eat them raw whenever possible.
- Avoid fruits canned in heavy syrup and canned vegetables in salt. Choose canned fruits in natural juices.
- Cook vegetables whole: they may cook faster if cut into small pieces, but the smaller you chop them, the more vitamins you lose. Potatoes baked in the oven will retain more vitamins than boiled potatoes.
- Store fruits and vegetables (except bananas), loosely wrapped, in the fridge and use as soon as possible.
- The next best to fresh are frozen vegetables. Vegetables stored for a few days after being picked have a similar nutrient content to frozen vegetables. However, if vegetables are stored for a week or longer they probably retain less nutrients than the frozen variety. Canned vegetables only retain about 50 per cent of their Vitamin C content.
- Two popular children's foods, baked beans and peas, are good sources of fibre. Try using the low-sugar variety of baked beans.

## VEGETARIAN DIET

For a vegetarian child, the two major sources of protein, meat and fish, are removed from the diet, so sometimes parents worry that their child is not going to get enough. However, eggs and milk are sources of high-quality protein as are soya products (tofu, soya milk and TVP, textured vegetable protein). Other sources of protein for vegetarians are seeds (sesame, sunflower, pumpkin), grains (wheat, barley, oats, rice etc.), pulses (lentils, peas, beans) and, for older children, nuts. Unlike animal proteins, plant proteins do not contain all the necessary amino acids, so you will need to include a wide variety of non-animal proteins in your child's diet. Whereas a good vegetarian diet rich in pulses, nuts and seeds is fine for children, problems arise when a child is given a non-meat diet which is *not* supplemented by these mineral- and protein-rich plant foods. It is important to ensure that children who are brought up as vegetarians are getting enough iron (see page 22), zinc and protein by regularly eating grains, seeds, nuts, beans, dairy products and eggs. These should be eaten with Vitamin C to help absorption.

A vegan diet excluding *all* animal protein can sometimes lead to problems as it's generally composed of relatively bulky foods, and young babies may not be able to consume enough food to obtain all the nutrients they need. Vegans will need a Vitamin B12 supplement as this particular vitamin is only found in animal foods. However, Vitamin B12 is present in breast milk and specially adapted infant formula. A strictly vegan diet for babies should only be undertaken with qualified guidance.

## DAIRY PRODUCTS

*Main nutrients provided:* **protein, calcium, fats, energy, Vitamins A and B**

Milk
Yoghurt and fromage frais

Cheese
Ice-cream

- Babies up to the age of six months should be having four to five milk feeds a day, and up to one year babies should have at least 600 ml (1 pint) of formula or breast milk each day. After one year, 400 ml (⅔ pint) of milk is adequate and you can change to cow's milk. Teenagers need about 600 ml (1 pint) of milk a day.

- Not only are dairy foods an excellent source of protein, but they are also the best source of calcium which is important for healthy bones and teeth. Calcium is particularly important for teenagers as almost half the adult bone mass is formed in adolescence. See page 24 for a list of foods high in calcium.
- Choose pasteurised whole-milk or semi-skimmed milk; semi-skimmed should only be given to children over the age of two (average or faddy eaters should continue with whole milk). Skimmed milk lacks the essential Vitamins A and D and is not a suitable food for young children who need the calories anyway unless they are overweight.
- Choose whole-milk yoghurts and dairy products unless your child is overweight. Many children prefer the flavoured types, but these contain sugar and sometimes colourings and preservatives. It's better to buy natural yoghurt and fromage frais and flavour it yourself with fresh fruit or fruit purées.
- If your child isn't keen on milk or dairy products, then try giving cream soups or milk-based desserts like fruits with custard or good quality ice-cream or frozen yoghurt made with natural ingredients and not too much sugar.

## MILK

Milk is more like a food than a drink and is the staple diet of most babies up to the age of one year. Milk is an excellent form of calcium and protein for young children, but too much milk can be harmful. Milk and dairy products are very poor sources of iron and zinc, and too much calcium can block iron and zinc absorption. If your child drinks too much milk, it will take his appetite away from other foods, and he may become deficient in both iron and zinc. Children between the age of one and five should have about 400 ml (⅔ pint) of milk each day or the equivalent in yoghurt or cheese etc. Many children with poor appetites drink excessive quantities of milk – up to 1.2 litres (2 pints) a day – so try to cut this down to 400 ml (⅔ pint) per day.

## MEAT AND MEAT ALTERNATIVES

**Main nutrients provided:** *protein, fat, B vitamins, energy and minerals. Vitamin B12, which is not found in foods of vegetable origin, is vital for healthy blood and nerves*

Meat
Fish
Poultry

Beans and lentils (chickpeas, butter beans etc.)
Nuts and nut products such as peanut butter
Eggs
Tofu

- It's reassuring to know that most of us eat more protein than we need, and that protein deficiency is almost unheard of in this country.
- A lot of people are turning away from eating red meat for health reasons. However, meat is an excellent source of protein, B vitamins, iron and zinc. Liver and kidneys are the best source of iron, so try and include these in your child's diet. They can be chopped and mixed with minced meat if your child doesn't fancy them on their own.
- Buy lean meat and trim off all visible fat. Meat products such as beefburgers and sausages are very fatty. Don't choose them too often and when you do, grill rather than fry them. Avoid processed meats, as these have a high fat and salt content and usually contain additives.
- Ready-minced meat is often very fatty. Ask your butcher to take some lean cuts of meat and mince them especially for you. Dry-fry mince without adding extra fat in a non-stick pan and pour off the excess fat before using.
- Chicken and turkey are low in fat so long as the skin is removed. Most of the fat is found just under the skin and will easily come away with it. The white meat contains less fat than the dark meat, but the dark meat contains more iron. Always cook chicken thoroughly because it can be contaminated with salmonella.

- Fish is an excellent low-fat source of protein, so try and encourage your child to eat more. Oily fish like mackerel, salmon, sardines and tuna are an excellent source of Vitamins A and D, and have been shown to protect against heart disease.
- Eggs supply protein, iron and zinc and are therefore an excellent food for your child. Do not serve raw or lightly cooked eggs to young children.
- All foods of animal origin are classified as 'complete' proteins. Most protein foods from plants are 'incomplete', lacking one or more of the essential amino acids, so the inclusion of some animal protein, such as milk, cheese or eggs, will ensure an adequate diet for vegetarians (see page 19).

## FATS

Coronary disease linked to unhealthy eating and a lack of exercise is the biggest cause of death in Britain, and recent research at the Great Ormond Street Hospital has shown that children as young as seven are showing early signs of heart disease. Much of this is due to fat intake.

There are two types of fat: saturated fat which comes mainly from animal sources, and unsaturated fat which comes from vegetable sources. Saturated fats can increase blood cholesterol levels, and high intakes are linked with an increased risk of heart disease. Try to limit *saturated* fat in your child's diet by choosing lean cuts of meat and trimming off any excess fat, and use liquid vegetable oils instead of hard fats for cooking. Grill and bake rather than fry. Fat, however, provides a concentrated supply of energy for young children, and children under the age of five should not be put on a low-fat diet unless they are overweight.

The small triangle at the top of the pyramid (on page 13) represents the fat in butter, margarine, low-fat spreads and cooking oils. Children need some fat in their diet, but many children ingest far more fat than they need, particularly if they eat a lot of junk food like hamburgers, pizza and chips. Dairy foods such as full-fat milk contain saturated fats, but they are also good sources of calcium, protein and vitamins.

SATURATED FATS
Meat
Butter
Lard and suet
Eggs
Cheese and full-fat yoghurt
Hard margarine
Hydrogenated vegetable fat or oil

UNSATURATED FATS
Sunflower oil
Soft margarine labelled 'high in
    polyunsaturates'
Corn oil
Olive oil
Rapeseed oil
Sesame oil
Safflower oil
Oily fish like mackerel, tuna or sardines

Vegetable oils like sunflower are good sources of Vitamin E which helps to maintain muscles, especially the heart, and also helps to prevent blood clots.

## SUGARS

The top of the pyramid (on page 13) represents the sugar found in confectionery, the sugar we add to foods and the sugar manufacturers add to foods such as soft drinks and juices, yoghurts, canned fruits, cakes and biscuits. These foods are simply empty calories taking away your child's appetite for more healthy foods, and therefore we should limit these foods in our child's diet. The more often these foods are eaten, the more likely it is, too, that our children will suffer tooth decay.

## SALT

Most of us eat more salt than we need, so try to cut down on salty foods like crisps. Too much salt can lead to high blood pressure which can increase the risk of a stroke or heart disease in later life and children who develop a taste for salty foods are likely to go on eating too much salt as adults. Use less salt in cooking and avoid adding salt at table.

## MINERALS

Deficiencies of vital nutrients can cause problems with your child's health and behaviour. These deficiencies are not uncommon because of the increased requirements during rapid growth and the fact that children are eating more and more processed foods from which many nutrients are lost in the refining process. However, if your child is healthy and has plenty of energy there is no need to worry.

If your child lacks energy or is frequently ill, it is important to be aware that good nutrition derives from a balance of nutrients – too much of one mineral may block the absorption of another. For example, calcium blocks zinc and iron absorption, so the result of too much milk or too many dairy products may be an iron or zinc deficiency. If your child is failing to thrive, consult your doctor or a nutritionist who may help you put together a more balanced diet for your child, or perhaps recommend a multi-vitamin supplement.

### IRON

Iron deficiency is the commonest nutritional problem in developed countries. It is particularly prevalent in children under five, and in teenage girls. A recent government survey into the diets of schoolchildren found that nearly every teenage girl in the UK has an average intake of iron which is below recommended levels and 25% of children in this country suffer from iron deficiency. Iron deficiency often remains unrecognised because symptoms are so subtle – pallor, listlessness, fatigue and reduced resistance to infection. Iron is crucial to brain functioning, and iron deficiency can affect a child's capacity to think and remember, and can impair mental development.

It is most important that babies receive breast milk or formula milk fortified with iron and vitamins until they are one year old. Vegetarian children should have fortified infant soya milk. Very poor eaters or children who refuse iron-rich foods could continue with formula or a follow-on formula (higher in iron) until the age of two.

Iron is best absorbed in the form in which it is found in red meat, and meat can itself enhance the absorption of iron from non-meat sources. Although 'Popeye the Sailor Man' did a lot for the popularity of spinach, the iron in spinach is in fact difficult to absorb. Children brought up on a vegetarian diet are three times more likely to be anaemic.

In order to increase the absorption of iron from plant sources, your child will need to consume a good Vitamin C source at the same meal, so serve Vitamin C rich fruits and vegetables with non-animal sources of iron. Many breakfast cereals are fortified with iron and including these for breakfast will help to increase your child's iron levels providing a source of Vitamin C is taken at the same meal. A good combination might be a bowl of iron-enriched cereal and a glass of orange juice. If your child is a vegetarian or eats little animal protein, do not give milk or tea with main meals as this reduces iron absorption.

The following are good sources of iron:

| | |
|---|---|
| Red meat | Dark green leafy vegetables |
| Liver | Wholegrain/fortified breakfast cereals |
| Oily fish | Dried fruit (especially apricots) |
| Egg yolk | Pulses |

## VITAMINS

Infants fed on formula milk do not need supplements provided they drink at least one pint of milk a day. Breastfed infants under six months do not need vitamin supplements provided the mother had a good diet during pregnancy. However, from six months infants receiving breast milk as their main drink should be given supplements of Vitamins A and D.

After one year, if your child is eating a reasonably well-balanced diet, he should be getting all the vitamins he needs, but if your child is a picky or faddy eater he should be given supplements of Vitamins A, D and C. Babies brought up on a vegan diet should take a Vitamin B12 supplement.

Recent research suggests that the antioxidant Vitamins E and C as well as Vitamin A in the form of beta-carotene (the pigment found in orange vegetables and fruits, and dark green vegetables) help to prevent certain forms of cancer and heart disease. Therefore encouraging a diet rich in fruits and vegetables, the natural sources of antioxidant vitamins, may well benefit your child's long-term health. Good sources are carrots, sweet potato, tomatoes, dark green vegetables like spinach, spring greens and broccoli, mango, cantaloupe melon and apricots.

## CALCIUM

Calcium is particularly important for good bones and teeth. Milk and dairy products are the main sources of calcium in our diet. Children between the ages of two and twelve should be drinking 400 ml (⅔ pint) of milk a day or should get the equivalent in dairy products. One pot of yoghurt and 25 g (1 oz) of hard cheese provide the same amount of calcium as 200 ml (⅓ pint) of milk. The following list is of foods rich in calcium:

| 100 g/4 oz | mg calcium per 100 g/4 oz | 100 g/4 oz | mg calcium per 100 g/4 oz |
|---|---|---|---|
| Parmesan cheese | 1200 | Whole milk yoghurt | 200 |
| Gruyère cheese | 950 | Low-fat yoghurt | 190 |
| Edam cheese | 750 | Spinach, boiled | 170 |
| Cheddar cheese | 740 | Dairy vanilla ice-cream | 130 |
| Sardines canned in oil | | Whole milk | 115 |
| (including bones) | 540 | Semi-skimmed milk | 120 |
| Tofu (soya bean curd) | 510 | | |

Adolescents need even more calcium than younger children or adults. That's because calcium is a major component of bones and almost half of your adult bone mass is formed during adolescence. It is recommended that boys between the ages of eleven and eighteen consume 1000 mg of calcium each day, and girls 800 mg.

---

### NUTS

Nuts can cause a severe allergic reaction. Where there is a history of food allergy, avoid all products containing nuts until the child is about three years old. Where there is no history of allergy, peanut butter can be given after the age of one. Any recipe containing nuts in this book is labelled with an **N**.

---

# CHAPTER TWO

# First Foods for Babies

A nte-natal classes seem to end abruptly at breast-feeding, and we are plunged into motherhood with next to no training, yet arguably this is the most responsible and important role a woman can perform. Since so many people will die prematurely from diet-related disease, it is vitally important that we give our babies the best possible start in life and set them on the road to a healthy eating pattern for the rest of their lives.

Despite the long lists of nutritional information on commercial baby foods, there is nothing to beat the taste and goodness of fresh home-made baby food. In just a couple of hours you can make a whole month's food supply for your baby and store it in the freezer, so you don't need to spend hours in the kitchen to give your baby the best start in life. Many commercial baby foods are poor value for money: ingredients are bulked out with water and thickeners, and more often than not you need to refer to the label to know what's inside. Also, babies who get used to processed foods often find it difficult to adapt to home-made foods later on. By making baby food at home, you know exactly what your baby is eating. There is an infinite variety and it works out much cheaper than feeding your baby from packets and jars. You probably don't eat from these yourself, so why should your baby?

Solids should be introduced some time between four and six months. If they are introduced earlier, a baby's digestive and immune systems are not sufficiently developed and there is more risk of your baby developing a food allergy, particularly if there is a family history.

Solids are important to get your baby used to different textures and tastes. Introducing a liking for healthy foods early on will lead to good eating habits as your child grows up. Puréed fruits and vegetables and sugar-free, vitamin- and iron-enriched baby rice are ideal first foods (rice is gluten-free, and therefore the best cereal if you want to avoid an allergy to cereal). Purées should be quite liquid in consistency to begin with, then, as your baby gets used to swallowing, you can decrease the amount of added liquid. Begin with single-ingredient purées and once your baby is used to a variety of different tastes you can start combining foods together. However, strong flavoured vegetables like broccoli or parsnip will go down better if they are mixed with rice or mashed potato. I have also found that mixing fruits with savoury foods can go down very well.

## PREPARING PURÉES

The best way to preserve the fresh taste and vitamins in vegetables and cooked fruits is to steam or microwave them or perhaps bake them in the oven (baked potatoes or apples for instance). It's worth investing in a multi-layered steamer to enable you to steam several foods at one time. Vitamins C and B are water-soluble, so if you are cooking in water, use as little as possible. Thoroughly wash or lightly scrape vegetables like courgettes, new potatoes or carrots rather than peel them as valuable vitamins lie just below the skin.

### HOW TO MAKE A VEGETABLE PURÉE     MAKES 10 ICE-CUBE PORTIONS

*350 g (12 oz) of any of the following: carrot, potato\*, swede, sweet potato, butternut squash, pumpkin or parsnip*
Scrape or peel the vegetables, rinse in a sieve, then chop into small pieces. Steam for 10–15 minutes or until soft. Alternatively put the vegetables in a saucepan and pour over some water from the kettle until just covered. Cover the pan and simmer for about 15 minutes or until soft. Blend the vegetable to a purée using some of the liquid from the bottom of the steamer or the pan. Spoon a little into a bowl for your baby's meal. Allow the remainder to cool down and once cool enough, freeze any extra portions.

   \*Potato should be puréed in a mouli (hand-turned food mill) or pressed through a sieve. Do not use a food processor, it breaks down the starches and produces a sticky pulp.

### HOW TO MAKE A FRUIT PURÉE     MAKES 6 ICE-CUBE PORTIONS

*2 medium apples or 2 ripe pears, 15–30ml (1–2 tbsp water)*
Choose a sweet variety of eating apple or pear. Peel, core and chop. Put into a heavy saucepan with the water, cover and cook over a low heat until tender (about 10 minutes for apples or 4 minutes for pears). Purée with an electric hand blender until smooth. Allow to cool down and freeze extra portions.

Fruits such as bananas and papayas do not require cooking provided they are ripe and can simply be puréed or mashed. You can add a little breast or formula milk if you like. These fruit purées cannot be frozen.

## STEAMING

Cook, covered, until tender but not mushy, then blend or mash very well. If the purée is too thick, you can add some of the water in the bottom of the steamer or a little milk to thin it down a little.

## MICROWAVING

Add a little water, cover and microwave in a suitable dish on full power until tender. Add enough water to make a smooth purée.

## BAKING

If you are cooking dinner in the oven for the rest of the family then you could take the opportunity to bake a potato or perhaps some pumpkin, sweet potato or squash. When soft, purée with some milk or water.

## BOILING

Use the minimum amount of water and be careful not to overcook fruits and vegetables. Add enough of the cooking liquid to make a smooth purée.

## FREEZING

Freeze foods as soon as possible once they have cooled down. For very young babies it is best to freeze foods in tiny quantities. An ice-cube tray is ideal for this. Once the cubes are frozen you can plop them out and transfer them to a freezer bag which you should label clearly with the expiry date. Fruit and vegetable purées will last for six months in a 4-star freezer, and fish, chicken and meat purées will last for four months. As your baby gets older you can freeze in larger portions.

Thaw foods by either taking them out of the freezer several hours before a meal, heating gently in a saucepan or defrosting in a microwave. Always reheat foods thoroughly and test the temperature of food before giving it to your baby. If reheating in a microwave, make sure that you stir the food to get rid of any hot spots.

Freezing can sometimes dry out foods so it may be necessary to add some liquid like milk or stock to get it back to the right consistency. If you have friends with babies roughly the same age, to save time you can each prepare different purées and share them between you. You can then each store a whole range of foods in your freezer. All recipes in this book that are suitable for freezing will be labelled with a ✳ sign.

# First Feeding Chart

| **4-5 MONTHS** Up to five months your baby should have at least four to five milk feeds a day. | **TEXTURE** Semi-liquid purées, no lumps or pips.<br>**FRUITS** Apple, pear, banana•, papaya•.<br>**VEGETABLES** Carrot, potato, sweet potato, swede, parsnip, pumpkin, courgette, squash (butternut squash is particularly good).<br>**CEREALS** Baby rice mixed with formula, breast milk or cooled boiled water. |
|---|---|
| **5-6 MONTHS**<br><br>• These fruits don't need to be cooked | **TEXTURE** Smooth purées, no lumps, pips or strings.<br>**FRUITS** Apricot, plum, peach•, melon•, kiwi•, avocado•.<br>Dried fruits: apricots, prunes (good mixed with baby rice and formula milk).<br>**VEGETABLES** Cauliflower, broccoli*, peas, green beans, sweet pepper*, tomato*.<br>*Mix these with other vegetables like potato or squash, or baby rice. |
| **6 MONTHS** Babies should have at least 600 ml (1 pint) milk each day up to the age of one year.<br><br><br><br><br>Don't add salt before one year. Try to sweeten foods with pure fruit juice rather than with sugar.<br>NB. Breast-fed babies may be short of iron, so iron-rich foods (see page 22) are particularly important. | **TEXTURE** Mashed, finely minced or puréed.<br>**DAIRY PRODUCTS** Can now use cow's milk in cooking and with breakfast cereal, but continue with formula (fortified with vitamins and iron) or breast milk for the first year. Introduce whole-milk yoghurts like Greek yoghurt (best to use natural yoghurts and sweeten with fresh fruit or fruit purées), fromage frais, cottage cheese and mild hard cheese.<br>**CHICKEN** Chopped or puréed chicken combines well with potato and tomato, apple, rice and tomato, avocado, carrots, squash, courgettes and apple juice.<br>**FISH** Plaice is ideal for very young babies as it makes a nice smooth purée. Combines well with cheese sauce, tomatoes and potato, spinach and cheese, grapes and white sauce. Also try cod, lemon sole, salmon and haddock.<br>**MEAT** Liver is an excellent food for babies. It is easily digested and rich in iron. Combines well with sautéed onions, mushrooms, tomatoes and potato. Lean minced beef cooked and then finely chopped in a food processor is good served with pasta and tomato sauce, rice or mashed potato. Slow-cooked casseroles with potato, onion and carrots can make tasty purées.<br>**CEREALS** Porridge, Ready Brek, Weetabix, wholemeal bread, rusks and rice cakes. |

| 6-7 MONTHS | **TEXTURE** Mashed, finely minced or puréed.<br>**FRUITS** Citrus fruits (remove pith and seeds), berry fruits (put through a hand mill to get rid of pips and seeds), mango, grapes (peel and deseed – do not give whole grapes).<br>**VEGETABLES** Onion, leek, cabbage, spinach, sweetcorn, mushrooms. |
|---|---|
| 8-9 MONTHS | **TEXTURE** Chopped, grated, coarser purées. Finger foods: sticks of raw or steamed vegetables.<br>**EGGS** Do not serve raw or lightly cooked eggs to young babies under 1 year. However, eggs are an excellent source of protein – try hard-boiled eggs, Spanish omelette, well-cooked scrambled eggs with cheese and tomato.<br>**BEANS AND PULSES** Lentils, split peas, butter beans, tofu.<br>**FISH** Oily fish such as mackerel and tuna, but avoid shellfish.<br>**CEREALS** Choose wholegrain cereals that are low in sugar and salt, such as: cornflakes, granola, muesli. |
| **10-12 MONTHS**<br><br>Every baby develops at her own pace, so use this chart as a guideline only, there are no hard and fast rules as to when to introduce new foods. Don't rush your baby, wait until she is ready to progress to the next stage. Formula or breast milk will provide most of the proteins, vitamins and minerals your baby needs for the first year. | **TEXTURE** Bite-sized pieces but avoid foods that might cause your child to choke: whole nuts or fruits with stones. Vary the consistency of foods from soups to finger foods.<br>**DAIRY PRODUCTS** Your baby still needs 600 ml (1 pint) whole milk each day, either in the form of formula or breast milk or dairy products like yoghurt or cheese. Solids should now be the major part of your child's diet, so cut down on any extra milk feeds if your baby is not eating well.<br>**SOLIDS** With the exception of raw or lightly cooked eggs, peanuts, shellfish and soft cheeses, your baby should be able to eat most foods. It is important to include iron-rich foods like red meat, dark green vegetables, lentils, egg yolk and iron-fortified cereals in your baby's diet as your baby will be changing to cow's milk from 1 year which, unlike formula milk, is not fortified with iron.<br>**COW'S MILK** After the first year, babies can drink pasteurised cow's milk. For children up to 2 years old, whole milk should be given because they need the energy and Vitamin A that the fat in the milk supplies. |

# QUANTITIES

Introduce a few spoonfuls of solids at just one meal to begin with, gradually moving to three or four solid meals each day by seven to eight months. The quantities will vary so be guided by your child's individual needs rather than be influenced by what other babies are eating. It is important to remember that the most important source of nutrition during the first year is milk. See the feeding chart on pages 28 and 29 to determine the appropriate quantity of milk for your baby's age.

# DRINKS

Babies and toddlers should not need to drink anything other than milk or cooled boiled water. Commercial baby drinks should be used sparingly and then only at mealtimes served in a cup. Baby drinks often contain concentrated fruit juices which encourage a sweet tooth and also cause tooth decay. Many children have damaged teeth as a result of drinking sweet drinks from their bottles.

# EQUIPMENT

You don't need lots of specialist equipment to prepare baby food. However it is worth investing in the following item:

- A hand-held electric blender which is excellent for puréeing small quantities.

- A hand-turned food mill (sometimes called a mouli). There are several available now which are specially designed to cope with baby food. They are good for puréeing food and at the same time getting rid of the indigestible parts like the husks of vegetables and the tough skins of dried fruits and pips or seeds.

- A multi-layered steamer. This can cook several foods at one time and will help preserve vitamins in cooked fruits and vegetables.

- Make sure all the utensils you use are thoroughly washed and wash your hands before preparing food for your baby. Sterilise spoons (or anything that goes into a baby's mouth) or wash it in a dishwasher.

# When Baby Says No!

Is your baby the kind that hardly eats, never seems hungry, won't try new foods and yet has boundless energy and seems perfectly healthy? Don't worry, you're not alone. Babies grow at a much slower rate after the age of one. While babies usually gain about fifteen pounds in their first year, they may only gain four or five pounds each year between the ages of one and five, so it's not surprising that their demand for food dwindles. Nearly every child goes through a phase of fussy eating: he may become fixed on eating just a few favourite foods or simply pick at food before pushing the plate away or flatly refuse to eat at mealtimes. The trouble is that very often the more we cajole our children to eat, the less likely they are to comply with our wishes and we become locked in a battle of wills which usually results in a very messy kitchen floor and a frustrated and bad-tempered Mum!

It's important to remember that this is a common stage and that your child will almost certainly grow out of it. Here are some suggestions you might like to try to make mealtimes a happier experience.

1. If your baby refuses her food, don't make a fuss, but leave the meal in front of her, and carry on eating your own meal. She will soon find that refusing food isn't so much fun if you don't react. She'll want to eat when she starts to feel hungry. It's best not to offer an alternative, or you'll find yourself emptying the contents of your larder at every mealtime.

2. Many children have a poor appetite at mealtimes because they have so many in-between snacks that they never feel truly hungry. Cut out 'junk food' like crisps, sweet biscuits and soft drinks and limit snacks to fresh fruit or raw vegetables, making sure they are given well before the next proper meal.

3. If your baby is drinking more than 900 ml (1½ pints) of milk a day, cut down on this and, if you haven't already, switch from a bottle to a cup. Encourage your child to drink water rather than fruit juices as these take away her appetite as well as being bad for her teeth. It may be an idea to offer a drink at the end of a meal rather than during the meal so

as not to spoil your child's appetite.

4. Put the fun back into mealtimes. Whenever possible, try to arrange for your baby to eat with the rest of the family or with some of her friends. It's always good for babies to see others enjoying eating, and of course food on other people's plates is often more enticing!

5. Offer small portions – piling food on a plate can put babies off and they'll soon let you know if they want more. Bright contrasting colours like a mixture of peas, sweetcorn and carrots look appealing. Children also like individual portions of food like mini fish pies so it's worth investing in some small ovenproof dishes like ramekins.

6. If your baby doesn't like drinking milk, offer her cheese or yoghurt, or use more milk in your cooking – make cauliflower cheese or add milk to soups, for example.

7. If your baby refuses a particular food, don't give up: children might dislike something one week and love it the next. A good idea is to combine foods your baby isn't so keen on with foods that she loves like chopped vegetables with pasta or minced meat with rice. A little disguise works wonders too, like adding carrots and green pepper to a tomato sauce and then blending it in a food processor. If your baby doesn't like chewing, you can change the texture of foods like chopping minced meat in a food processor or combining chopped chicken with vegetables and a cheese sauce and forming the mixture into little sausages.

8. Try to make food more fun to eat, and allow your baby to feed herself if she wants to. Prepare some suitable food like sticks of raw vegetables and fingers of toast and encourage her to dunk them in a delicious dip made with some good nutritious ingredients. Simple things like arranging fruit in the shape of a face on her plate can work wonders.

9. Be careful over the timing of meals. If meals are too close together, your child may not be hungry, and if her last meal of the day is late, she may be too tired.

10. Try to make sure that there aren't too many distractions at feeding time like television or other children running around the kitchen, and try to give your baby lots of attention.

11. Involve your child in preparing the meal. Maybe take her shopping and let her choose her own fruits and vegetables. Older children will enjoy helping in the preparation, and they're much more likely to enjoy eating foods that they've had a hand in preparing.

# Weaning Winners

The recipes in this section can be made into soups or baby purées, or a combination, so that you can cook for the family and your baby at the same time. The only difference is that you should not add salt to baby food, and if you want to make fairly thick baby purées, you will need to add less stock or milk.

# Real Chicken Stock

Blend together this delicious home-made chicken stock and some of the cooked boiled chicken used in the stock to make a tasty and nutritious purée for your baby.

*⁕ From 4 months*

MAKES 1.75 LITRES (3 PINTS)

1 large boiling chicken cut into quarters, plus giblets, or the carcass of a cooked roast chicken plus giblets

1 veal knuckle (optional)

2.25 litres (4 pints) water

2 large onions, roughly chopped

3 large carrots, roughly chopped

2 leeks, white part only, sliced

1 large parsnip, peeled and roughly chopped

½ celery stick with some leaves

1 sprig parsley or dried parsley

1 bay leaf

10 ml (2 tsp) tomato purée

2 chicken stock cubes, crumbled (optional)

a little freshly ground black pepper

For maximum flavour, make chicken stock from a boiling chicken with its giblets. Ask your butcher to order one for you if he doesn't usually have them. The chicken joints can be lifted out when tender (after about 2 hours), the flesh removed and reserved for later use, and the chicken bones returned to the pan for a further 1½–2 hours. Otherwise, use the cooked carcass from a roast chicken with as many giblets as possible. These can be stockpiled in the freezer when cooking a roast chicken or making a chicken casserole. I like to add a veal knuckle to the stock as they improve the flavour, so ask your butcher to keep some for you.

Wash the chicken joints, veal knuckle and giblets, or break up the carcass if you are using this instead of a boiling chicken. Put in a large pan and cover with the water. Bring to the boil slowly and with a flat metal spoon, remove any scum from the surface. Add all the remaining ingredients and simmer very gently for 3½–4 hours, either in the oven at 150°C/300°F/Gas 2 or on top of the stove. If you are using a boiling chicken, strip the flesh from the bones after 2 hours. Set aside for use in other recipes and return the bones to the pan.

Allow to cool and refrigerate overnight. In the morning, you will be able to remove the layer of fat that settles on the surface. Strain the stock and discard the vegetables and bones. Ideally, make this in large batches and freeze it in 300 ml (½ pint) containers.

*Variations:* to make CHICKEN NOODLE SOUP, simply add some cooked vermicelli and some cooked vegetables – thin strips of carrots or little broccoli florets, for instance – to some of the strained stock. You could also add some diced chicken from the boiling fowl. If your child prefers, you could use cooked rice instead of noodles.

To make VEGETABLE STOCK, roughly chop a large onion, carrot and leek, and sauté in 25 g (1 oz) butter or margarine, for 10 minutes. Add some parsley, a bay leaf, a few peppercorns and maybe a few extra vegetables or trimmings such as mushrooms, cabbage or celery. Pour over 1.5 litres (2½ pints) cold water, bring to the boil, skim, reduce heat and simmer for about 45 minutes. Sieve through a strainer, pressing on the vegetables with the back of a spoon to extract their juices. Bring the stock back to the boil and reduce to get a better flavour. Allow to cool, refrigerate and remove any fat from the surface.

# Cherub's Chowder

Babies love the sweet taste of sweetcorn. The trouble is that, when it is made into a purée, the husks tend to be a bit lumpy and difficult to digest, so for young babies I prefer to put it through a mouli. For older babies, I purée the potato mixture and then stir in the sweetcorn whole.

❋ *From 6 months*
MAKES 5 PORTIONS

1 onion, chopped

15 ml (1 tbsp) vegetable oil

1 medium potato (225 g/8 oz), peeled and cut into cubes

175 ml (6 fl oz) vegetable or chicken stock (see pages 34 or 35)

50 g (2 oz) fresh or frozen sweetcorn

60 ml (2 fl oz) milk

50 g (2 oz) cooked chicken, diced

Sauté the chopped onion in the oil until soft. Add the potato, and pour over the stock. Bring to the boil, then cover and simmer for about 12 minutes. Add the sweetcorn and the milk and simmer for a further 2–3 minutes. Purée the soup in a mouli together with the chicken and heat through. Alternatively, for older babies, purée the onion and potato mixture in a mouli, stir in the sweetcorn whole and the finely chopped chicken. Add a little extra milk and stock to make this into soup.

# See in the Dark Soup

This recipe makes six portions of baby purée but if you want to turn this into a delicious soup simply add 450 ml (¾ pint) chicken or vegetable stock and the juice of half an orange.

Sauté the onion in the butter until softened. Add the carrots and sauté for 3–4 minutes. Pour over the stock, bring to the boil, then reduce the heat and simmer for about 20 minutes or until the carrots are tender. Add the orange juice and purée in a blender.

✳ *From 5 to 6 months*
MAKES 6 PORTIONS (of purée)
1 small onion, sliced
25 g (1 oz) butter or margarine
450 g (1 lb) carrots, thinly sliced
300 ml (½ pint) chicken or
  vegetable stock (see pages 34
  or 35)
juice of ½ orange

# Courgette and Potato Purée

This has a lovely fresh flavour, but make sure the courgettes are firm, otherwise they can have a bitter taste. Simply increase the quantities and add more stock to make a delicious soup for the whole family. Once your baby is older you can try mashing food instead of puréeing it.

✳ *From 8 months*

MAKES 6 PORTIONS

½ small onion, chopped

20 g (¾ oz) butter or margarine

1 large potato (about 300 g/10 oz), peeled and cut into small chunks

200 ml (7 fl oz) chicken or vegetable stock (see pages 34 or 35)

1 large courgette (about 150 g/ 5 oz), topped, tailed and sliced

Sauté the onion in butter until softened, add the potato and continue to cook for 2–3 minutes. Pour over the chicken or vegetable stock, bring to the boil and then simmer, covered, for 5 minutes. Add the sliced courgette and simmer for about 15 minutes or until the courgettes are tender. Mash everything together with a potato masher.

# Lovely Lentils

Lentils are a good source of protein and beta-carotene and also provide folate, fibre and Vitamin C. Orange-fleshed sweet potato is an excellent source of beta-carotene and makes a sweet, soft, smooth purée that appeals to young babies. Add extra stock for a delicious warming soup for the family.

M elt the butter in a saucepan and sauté the leeks for 2 to 3 minutes. Add the celery, red pepper and carrot and sauté for 5 minutes. Add the lentils, sauté for one minute, then add the sweet potato and bay leaf and pour over 450 ml (15 fl oz) of stock. Bring to the boil, then reduce the heat, cover and simmer for about 30 minutes, or until the vegetables and lentils are tender. Remove the bay leaf and blend to a purée. Return to the pan, stir in 300 ml (½ pint) more stock, heat through and season to taste to make a delicious soup.

✳ *From 7 months*

MAKES 12 PORTIONS BABY PURÉE

30 g (1 oz) butter

125 g (4 oz) leeks, finely sliced

30 g (1 oz) celery, chopped

30 g (1 oz) red pepper, cored, de-seeded and chopped

100 g (4 oz) 1 medium carrot, peeled and chopped

60 g (2 oz) red lentils

275 g (10 oz) sweet potato, peeled and chopped

1 bay leaf

450 ml (15 fl oz) + 300 ml (½ pint) vegetable stock (see page 35)

# Bravo Barley Soup

I remember as a child loving the thick barley soup that my mother made. My version is less thick because my children prefer it that way, but you could try increasing the amount of barley so that it becomes more like a sort of risotto but with barley instead of rice.

❈ *From 8 months*

MAKES 8 PORTIONS

1 onion, chopped

15 ml (1 tbsp) vegetable oil

100 g (4 oz) carrots, diced

½ celery stick, diced

40 g (1½ oz) pearl barley (well rinsed)

1.5 litres (2½ pints) chicken or vegetable stock (see pages 34 or 35)

50 g (2 oz) French beans, topped, tailed and cut into short lengths

2 medium tomatoes, skinned and chopped

a handful of parsley, chopped

a little salt and freshly ground black pepper (not before 1 year)

Sauté the onion in the oil until softened but not coloured. Add the carrot and celery and cook gently for about 10 minutes. Add the barley and pour over the stock. Cover and simmer for 35 minutes or until the barley is just tender. Add the beans, tomatoes and parsley, season to taste, and simmer for a further 10 minutes.

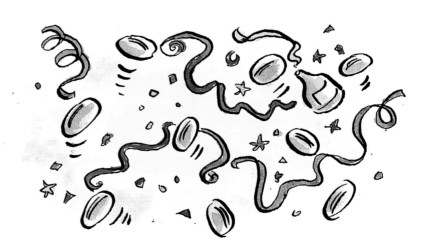

# Tomato Soup with Macaroni and Meatballs

A lovely home-made tomato soup with the added attraction of pasta. Break up the meatballs and mash them into the soup for young babies.

To make the meatballs mix together all the ingredients except for the oil. Using your hands, form into small balls (you should get about 20), then sauté in a little oil until browned and just cooked through (they will be cooked again in the soup).

For the soup, sauté the onion and carrots in the olive oil until soft, then stir in the undrained tomatoes, the tomato paste and stock. Cover and simmer for 15 minutes, then blend in a food processor; strain to get rid of the tomato seeds. Stir in the pasta and meatballs, bring to the boil and then simmer, uncovered, for 6–7 minutes, or until the pasta is tender. Stir in the cream at the last minute.

✳ *From 8 months*

MAKES 8 PORTIONS

MEATBALLS

225 g (8 oz) lean minced beef

½ onion, finely chopped

a handful of parsley, chopped

30 ml (2 tbsp) breadcrumbs

½ egg yolk, beaten

½ teaspoon Marmite

vegetable oil for frying

SOUP

1 onion, finely chopped

75 g (3 oz) carrots, chopped

15 ml (1 tbsp) olive oil

1 x 800 g (28 oz) can of tomatoes

22.5 ml (1½ tbsp) tomato paste

900 ml (1½ pints) chicken stock (see page 34)

75 g (3 oz) small macaroni

45 ml (3 tbsp) double cream

41

# The Best Finger Foods

By the time your child is one year old, he should be able to cope with most foods. The difficulty comes when he no longer wishes to avail himself of Mum's personalised service of spoon-feeding and he decides that food will not enter his mouth unless he himself puts it there.

The best way to encourage your child to eat is to prepare foods that he can easily pick up with his fingers. His aim at this tender age is probably far from perfect and although it is good to encourage your child to use a spoon, serious eating is probably best done with his fingers. Below is a list of suitable finger foods. A good way to serve them is to put a selection into an empty ice-cube tray and refrigerate until needed. Your baby will have fun trying out all the different foods. (It's also a good idea to put a plastic tablecloth under the high chair so that you can re-cycle foods that get lost en route!)

On the next few pages are simple, easy-to-prepare recipes for delicious finger foods to tempt even the stubbornest little eaters. Chewing on finger foods will also help the formation of your child's teeth and gums, and will help soothe him while teething, particularly if they are cold. Whole nuts should not be given to children under the age of five because of the risk of choking. Chopped nuts can be given from two years and smooth nut butters are fine from 4–6 months.

*Never leave young babies alone whilst eating because of the possibility of them choking. If your child should choke, hold him face down over your arm or knee and give him four sharp slaps between the shoulder blades to dislodge the object. Remove any remaining morsels from your child's mouth with your fingers.*

# Finger Favourites

- Peeled raw fruits such as: banana, seedless grapes, blueberries, clementines, peach etc. Hard fruits like apples are best given in reasonably large pieces that your baby can hold and chew. Smaller pieces might be swallowed whole and cause choking. *Always remove fruit stones.*

- Dried fruit. These may need to be soaked in hot water if they are hard.

- Cooked vegetables like peas and sweetcorn. Corn on the cob when your child has enough teeth to chew on the corn.

- Sticks of raw vegetables, possibly with a dip. Grated vegetables. It's fun to arrange vegetables on a plate in the shape of a face – see Funny Faces, page 152.

- Cooked pasta with a fairly thick sauce which clings to the pasta.

- Pieces of cooked chicken.

- Chopped up hamburger or small meatballs.

- Wholegrain cereals without milk: puffed wheat, Rice Krispies, cornflakes, Oat Krunchies.

- Pieces of flaked white fish or tuna fish.

- Rice cakes or wholemeal biscuits.

- Cheese cut into fingers or grated.

- Miniature sandwiches with a soft filling: smooth peanut butter **N**, mashed banana, cottage cheese or Marmite, or finger-sized pitta breads with soft fillings.

- Hard-boiled eggs.

- Fingers of toast (soldiers!) with a dip like houmous or make your own dip – simply mix mashed avocado with chopped tomatoes, cream cheese and chives.

- Mini salads with skinned, seeded tomatoes, slices of cucumber, grated carrot or cheese etc.

- Fingers of cheese on toast or pizza (choose from a large selection in the 'Healthy Fast Food' section on page 137).

# Sesame Fish Fingers

A tasty home-made version of fish fingers. You can marinate the fish in some lemon juice and garlic before cooking to add flavour. Crushed cornflakes make another good coating for fish. These are good served with chips and ketchup.

❋ *From 9 months*
MAKES 6 FINGERS

175 g (6 oz) white fish, filleted
   and skinned (cod, haddock,
   plaice, lemon sole)

15 g (½ oz) sesame seeds

50 g (2 oz) fine matzo meal

a little salt and freshly ground
   black pepper (not before
   1 year)

plain flour for coating

1 egg, beaten

15 ml (1 tbsp) vegetable
   oil

Cut the fish into six fingers. Mix together the sesame seeds, matzo meal and seasoning. Lightly coat each piece of fish in flour, dip in the egg and then roll in the matzo meal and sesame mixture. Fry in the oil until golden and cooked through.

# Lara's Little Salmon Rissoles

These salmon rissoles are really delicious and very quick to prepare. They are also good cold and I think adults will like them too! Served with baby carrots and peas they will make a complete meal of finger food.

Flake the salmon checking carefully to make sure there are no bones. In a mixing bowl combine the salmon, grated onion, ketchup and matzo meal. Form into small rissoles and coat in matzo meal. Heat the oil in a frying pan and sauté the rissoles for about 2 minutes each side or until golden.

✳ *From 9 months*
MAKES 6 SMALL RISSOLES
1 x 213 g  (7½ oz) tin red salmon
18 g (1 heaped tbsp) grated onion
30 ml (2 tbsp)  tomato ketchup
12 g (1 tbsp)  fine matzo meal
   plus 25 g (1 oz) matzo meal for
   coating
30 ml (2 tbsp) vegetable oil

# Chicken and Potato Rissoles

The mashed potato makes these lovely and soft for your baby to eat. For variation, try adding cooked diced vegetables like broccoli or maybe some cooked frozen peas. Coating the rissoles in crushed wheat crackers gives them a lovely flavour.

✳ *From 9 months*

MAKES 16 RISSOLES

450 g (1 lb) potatoes, peeled and cut into chunks

225 g (8 oz) chicken breast, off the bone, or 175 g (6 oz) cooked chicken breast

22.5 ml (1½ tbsp) vegetable oil

1 onion, finely chopped

1 egg yolk

1 tablespoon milk

a handful of parsley, chopped

2.5 ml (½ tsp) dried mixed herbs

a little salt and freshly ground black pepper (not before 1 year)

wheat crackers, crushed with a rolling pin, or fine breadcrumbs

about 25 g (1 oz) butter or margarine, melted

Boil the potatoes until tender. Sauté the chicken in the oil until cooked through (unless you are using pre-cooked chicken), then remove from the pan. Sauté the onion until soft. Chop the chicken and onion in a food processor for a few seconds. Mash the cooked potatoes together with the egg yolk and milk, making sure there are no lumps, then mix in the chopped chicken and onion, the parsley and herbs. Season to taste and using your hands shape into about sixteen rissoles. Roll in the crushed wheat crackers or breadcrumbs, brush with melted butter or margarine and bake on a greased tray in an oven preheated to 180°C/350°F/Gas 4 for about 10 minutes. Alternatively, sauté the rissoles in butter or oil until golden.

# Mini Chicken Burgers with Apple

These are lovely and moist with a crisp coating, and the apple gives a flavour that children love. They are also good served cold, and are excellent for lunchboxes or picnics.

Squeeze some of the liquid from the grated onion, potato and apple. Combine with the chicken in a food processor, add the rest of the ingredients, except for the tomato ketchup, matzo meal and oil, and chop for a couple of seconds (do not chop too finely). Stir in the ketchup and 2 tablespoons of the matzo meal. Season to taste for babies of one year and older. With your hands, form into the shape of mini burgers, about fifteen, and roll in matzo meal. Fry in a little oil until golden and cooked through.

❋ *From 9 months*

MAKES ABOUT 15 MINI BURGERS

1 small onion, grated

1 medium potato, peeled and grated (about 150 g/5 oz)

1 Granny Smith apple, peeled, cored and grated

2 chicken breasts, skinned and cut into chunks

1 chicken stock cube, crumbled

22.5 ml (1½ tbsp) tomato ketchup

a handful of parsley, chopped

freshly ground black pepper (not before one year)

40 g (1½ oz) fine matzo meal

vegetable oil or margarine

# Annabel's Chicken Kebabs

These are finger licking good and you could add a few chunks of pineapple to the skewers if you like. These are also good cooked on a barbecue in summer and make a good meal served with rice and vegetables.

*From 1 year*

MAKES 4 PORTIONS

1 large chicken breast cut into
   bite-sized chunks or 3 large
   boned chicken thighs trimmed of
   fat and cut into chunks

MARINADE

½ small onion, finely chopped

15 ml (1 tbsp) vegetable oil

30 ml (2 tbsp) tomato ketchup

15 ml (1 tbsp) pineapple juice

5 ml (1 tsp) white wine vinegar

7.5 ml (1½ tsp) light soy sauce

5 ml (1 tsp) honey

Soak four 15 cm (6 in) bamboo skewers in water to prevent them getting scorched. To make the marinade, sauté the onion in the oil until soft, then add the rest of the marinade ingredients and simmer for 2–3 minutes or until the sauce thickens. Marinate the chunks of chicken for 1 hour or longer. Thread the chunks of chicken onto the pre-soaked skewers and cook in an oven preheated to 190°C/375°F/Gas 5 for 7 minutes each side, basting occasionally or until the chicken is cooked through.

Remove the chicken from the skewers for babies and very young children and cut into small pieces.

# Mini Beef and Veggie Burgers

The potato, carrot and apple makes these mini burgers moist and very tasty.

Boil the potato for 5 minutes, drain, cool and grate. Mix together all the ingredients except the flour, and with lightly floured hands, form the mixture into about fifteen mini burgers (about 5 cm/2 inches in diameter). Cook under a preheated grill for about 5 minutes each side.

❋ *From 1 year*

MAKES 15 BURGERS

1 medium potato, peeled and halved

½ small onion, grated

225 g (8 oz) lean minced beef

1 small carrot, grated

1 apple, peeled and grated

15 ml (1 tbsp) tomato ketchup

2.5 ml (½ tsp) Marmite

a little plain flour

# CHAPTER THREE

# Healthy Eating for Life

In early childhood, eating habits and tastes are formed for life, so set them on the right road to a lifelong healthy eating pattern.

A t a time when diet is a most critical factor to our well-being, it often tends to be overlooked in our busy lives when we turn to convenience foods for our children, with most meals emanating from jars, cans or packets. In this chapter, you'll find a host of easy-to-prepare, tried and tested meals full of good healthy ingredients. Your family *will* come back for seconds!

## BETTER BREAKFASTS

Nutritionists say that breakfast is the most important meal of the day, and a recent study in schools showed that the effects of an inadequate breakfast were quite pronounced – concentration suffered, children made more mistakes, worked more slowly and felt more tired. Empty calories are no good at all, your child needs lashings of energy from a nourishing breakfast. Many cereals designed specifically for children contain over 50 per cent sugar. Not only are these bad for your children's teeth, but the high level of sugar can cause blood sugar levels to rise quickly and then fall, leaving your child feeling tired and listless.

In this section I have given recipes and ideas to set your child up for the day ahead. A good breakfast could well make all the difference to your child's performance at school. You don't need to be rigid about what foods to serve. If your child fancies baked beans on toast or a slice of the Spanish omelette left over from yesterday, that would make an excellent breakfast.

*Remember that lightly cooked eggs should not be given to babies under one year.*

# Breakfast Tips

Recommended breakfast cereals

Corn flakes
Bran flakes and oat bran flakes
Ready Brek
Shredded Wheat
Rice Krispies
Shreddies
Multi Cheerios
Muesli (check sugar level)
Puffed Wheat
Weetabix
Special K

Cereals which have a high level of sugar

Frosties
Sugar Puffs
Coco Pops
Ricicles
Sugar Smacks
Lucky Charms

1. Adding fresh fruits or dried fruits like chopped dried apricots to breakfast cereals will give sweetness without the need for sugar. For example:

- Weetabix covered with sliced bananas and strawberries or grated apple
- Porridge with dried apricot purée or stewed apple and sultanas
- Shreddies with raisins and chopped apple
- Muesli with grapes, peaches and bananas

2. Fromage frais mixed with low-sugar jam, dried or fresh fruit purée makes a good spread.
3. A bowl of hot porridge makes a great start to a cold winter's day. Try adding fresh, seasonal fruit toppings or cook the porridge with chopped dried fruits like apricots.

Alternatively add one of these to the bowl of cooked porridge to make a change from honey or jam:

- Cooked fresh fruits

- Fruits canned in their own juice

- A small carton of fruit-flavoured fromage frais

- Chopped, ready-to-eat dried apricots

4. Greek yoghurt mixed with your child's favourite muesli and fresh fruit.

5. A circle of fresh berries surrounding Greek yoghurt topped with a sprinkling of brown sugar and your child can have fun dipping the fruit into the yoghurt.

6. Toaster French Toast: following the recipe on page 54, make the French toast in advance and reheat in the toaster.

7. Breakfast Sundae: into a sundae glass, spoon layers of yoghurt, fresh fruit (like mixed berries) and crunchy breakfast cereal.

8. Glazed Grapefruit: cut the grapefruit in half, cut around the edges and sections to loosen the grapefruit segments and drizzle with runny honey or maple syrup. Cook under a preheated grill (not too close or it may burn) until golden. Place a cherry in the centre before serving.

9. Dried fruit compotes are delicious served cold for breakfast. It's also nice to mix in some fresh fruits like apples, pears or oranges with the dried fruits. Add these towards the end of the cooking time as they will cook much faster. Fresh fruit purées like a combination of apple and pear are excellent for breakfast, particularly if your child is lazy at chewing.

10. Cottage cheese mixed with chopped fresh or dried fruits is good for breakfast. Serve plain or with fingers of toast.

11. Scrambled Eggs Plus: make scrambled eggs extra special by adding something from the list below or try a combination like broccoli and cheese.

- Skin, seed and chop tomatoes, and add about 30 seconds before the eggs are done.

- Steam or boil small broccoli florets and add 1 minute before the eggs are done.

- Sauté thinly sliced button mushrooms in butter and add about 30 seconds before the eggs are done.

- Add grated cheese like Cheddar, Edam or Gruyère about 1 minute before the eggs are done.

- Add some chopped avocado about 30 seconds before the eggs are done.

12. Omelettes with various fillings; for example, grated cheese and chopped tomato, diced ham or sweetcorn.

13. If your child is reluctant to eat at breakfast time, you might want to try making some nutritious fresh fruit smoothies or milkshakes. An electric hand blender is ideal for this.

Use apple, pineapple or grape juice as a base for the smoothies. You will need about 175 ml (6 fl oz) juice (1 small carton) for each piece of fruit. Here are some suggestions but it's easy to make up your own combinations.

- 100–125 g (4 oz) mango, 3 strawberries, 1 small banana, 1 orange squeezed

- 1 ripe juicy peach, 1 small banana, 1 orange squeezed

- 1 small pot vanilla yoghurt, 1 small banana, 120 ml (4 fl oz) milk, 7.5 ml (1½ tsp) honey and a sprinkling of toasted wheatgerm

For the milkshakes, strawberries, bananas, nectarines and peaches are some of the many fruits that can be used. Allow 100–175 g (4–6 oz) fruit per 300 ml (½ pint) of milk. Simply blend the fruit and milk together. For a richer milkshake, you could add a scoop of ice-cream.

# Funny Shape French Toast

There are lots of interesting biscuit cutters you can use – animal shapes, numbers, letters, stars or hearts for example. Your child will enjoy giving you a hand cutting out the bread, and getting children involved in the preparation usually works wonders for their appetite.

*From 1 year*
MAKES 6 SHAPES
3 slices bread
1 egg, beaten
30 ml (2 tbsp) milk
25 g (1 oz) butter

Cut the bread into your chosen shapes, two per slice. Beat together the egg and milk and pour into a shallow dish. Dip the bread shapes into the mixture and fry in butter until golden.

# Welsh Rarebit

A really tasty, nutritious breakfast to set your child up for the day.

Melt the butter in a small saucepan, add the cheese, milk or beer and the mustard and stir over a gentle heat until the cheese has melted and the mixture is smooth. Remove from the heat and beat in the egg yolk. Preheat the grill and arrange the hot toast on a sheet of foil on the grill pan. Spoon the mixture on to the slices of toast and sprinkle with a little paprika before placing under the grill for 3–4 minutes or until golden. Cut into fingers and serve.

*From 1 year*
MAKES 2 PORTIONS

10 g (¼ oz) butter

50 g (2 oz) Cheddar cheese, grated

15 ml (1 tbsp) milk or beer

a pinch of mustard powder

½ egg yolk, beaten

1 large or 2 small slices wholemeal toast

a little mild paprika

# Stewed Apples with Summer Fruits

Combinations of stewed fruit for breakfast are delicious and this one looks great too because everything turns a deep red colour. This can also be mixed together with a mild natural yoghurt and maybe some granola on top.

❋ *From 1 year*
MAKES 4 PORTIONS
400 g (14 oz) cooking apples
225 g (8 oz) frozen summer fruits
   (strawberries, raspberries,
   blueberries, cherries)
30 ml (2 tbsp) soft brown sugar

Put the apples and frozen berries into a saucepan together with the sugar. Cook, covered, over a low heat for 7 to 8 minutes. Once cool, put in the fridge.

# Apple and Carrot Muffins

Muffins make good portable food for breakfast on the run, lunchboxes or snacks away from home. They are simple to make but the result is irresistible. Home-baked muffins presented in a little basket lined with some gingham make a lovely present for teachers at the end of term.

In a large bowl mix together the first seven ingredients. In another bowl sift together the flours, baking powder, baking soda, salt, cinnamon and ginger. Gently fold the flour mixture into the wet mixture, taking care not to over-mix. Finally fold in the nuts (if using) and the raisins. Spoon into a prepared muffin tray lined with paper cases and bake in an oven preheated to 180°C/350°F/Gas 4 for 25–30 minutes.

✳ *From 1 year*

MAKES 12 MUFFINS

120 ml (4 fl oz) vegetable oil

3 eggs, lightly beaten

50 g (2 oz) soft brown sugar

50 g (2 oz) caster sugar

2 carrots, grated (about 90 g/ 3½ oz)

2 apples, peeled and grated

5 ml (1 tsp) pure vanilla extract

90 g (3½ oz) wholemeal flour

100 g (4 oz) self-raising flour

15 ml (1 tbsp) baking powder

2.5 ml (½ tsp) baking soda

2.5 ml (½ tsp) salt

2.5 ml (½ tsp) ground cinnamon

2.5 ml (½ tsp) ground ginger

40 g (1½ oz) pecans, finely chopped (optional)

75 g (3 oz) raisins

# Scrumptious Wholemeal Pancakes

My children's favourite breakfast would be these pancakes served warm with sliced bananas and a drizzle of maple syrup. You can prepare the batter and leave it in the fridge overnight and it will only take a few minutes to make the pancakes in the morning. They are also good served with blueberries, peaches or strawberries or, as they are so delicious, just serve them plain. You can stack the cooked pancakes with greaseproof paper between them and reheat in the oven. Alternatively, you can freeze them stored in a rigid plastic container interwoven with freezer layering paper to enable you to take one or two out at a time. Pancakes are also great for dessert served with fruit and vanilla ice-cream.

✳ *From 1 year*

MAKES ABOUT 12 PANCAKES

50 g (2 oz) wholemeal flour

50 g (2 oz) plain flour

5 ml (1 tsp) baking powder

2.5 ml (½ tsp) salt

8 g (2 tsp) soft brown sugar

1 egg, lightly beaten

2.5 ml (½ tsp) pure vanilla extract

15 g (½ oz) unsalted butter, melted

250 ml (8 fl oz) milk

vegetable oil

Sift together the flours, baking powder and salt, and stir in the sugar. Make a hollow in the centre and add the beaten egg, vanilla and melted butter. Gradually mix in the milk to make a smooth batter. Cover the bowl and set aside for an hour, or overnight in the fridge. Heat a little oil in an 18 cm (7 inch) frying pan, tilting the pan gently to coat the base and sides. Pour off any excess oil and use a ladle to pour in just enough batter to coat the base of the pan thinly. Cook for 1–2 minutes or until the underside is golden, then turn or toss and cook the other side.

# Meatless Meals

'Eat up your vegetables or you won't get any dessert' is a threat used by many a mother, but instead of a means to an end, why not make your child's vegetables more exciting? Try some fun ways with vegetables like fairy toadstools or delicious, crunchy, vegetable stir-fries.

Often children who don't like cooked vegetables enjoy eating them raw, so if you're despairing because Johnny won't eat his carrots and greens, dishing up tempting salads may well be your answer.

Of course, for some children refusing food is a way of asserting their independence, so why not offer three vegetables and then let them choose which two they would like to eat?

# Can't Resist Couscous

Couscous is a form of grain made from wheat and you can find it in most supermarkets next to the rice section. It's fairly high in minerals and vitamins and has a mild taste and wonderful soft texture perfect for babies, so if you have never tried it, give it a go and you may well find that your baby loves it too. You can combine it with all sorts of different vegetables. Aubergine, courgette and tomato make a good combination so if you're making a ratatouille for the rest of the family, set aside a small portion, chop the vegetables into little pieces and mix with some couscous which has been soaked in stock for a tasty and nutritious meal for your baby.

*From 8 months*
MAKES 3 PORTIONS

75 g (3 oz) quick-cooking couscous

175 ml (6 fl oz) vegetable stock (see page 35)

25 g (1 oz) carrot, sliced

25 g (1 oz) courgette, sliced (or frozen peas)

Pour the boiling stock over the couscous, stir with a fork and set aside for about 6 minutes by which time it will have absorbed the stock. Meanwhile, steam the carrot for about 4 minutes, add the courgette slices (or frozen peas) and steam for 2–3 minutes. Dice the cooked vegetables. Fluff the couscous with a fork and mix in the diced vegetables.

# I Like Brown Rice

If your child doesn't like any of the vegetables in the rice you can leave them out or substitute something that he does like.

Rinse the rice and drain. Heat 25 g (1 oz) of the butter in a large saucepan and sauté the onion until softened. Add the carrots and sauté for one minute.

Add the rice and toss to coat. Pour over the stock, bring to the boil, then cover and cook over a medium heat for 10 minutes. Add the diced courgette and cook for 5 minutes. Stir in the frozen peas and cook for 5 minutes. If necessary add a little more stock. Meanwhile, melt the remaining butter in a pan and sauté the sliced mushrooms for 3–4 minutes, then add 5 ml (1 tsp) of the soy sauce. Stir the mushrooms into the rice together with the remaining soy sauce.

✳ *From 9 months*
MAKES 4 PORTIONS
225 g (8 oz) easy cook brown rice
1 small onion, finely chopped
40 g (1½ oz) butter
100 g (4 oz) diced carrot
600 ml (1 pint) vegetable or
  chicken stock
100 g (4 oz) diced courgette
100 g (4 oz) sliced button
  mushrooms
50 g (2 oz) frozen peas
10 ml (2 tsp) soy sauce

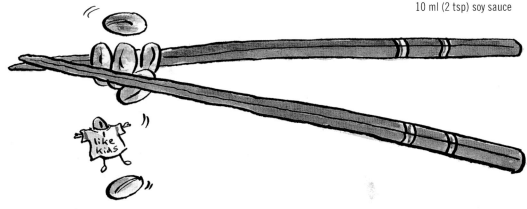

# Scarlett's Pearl Barley Risotto

Unlike a traditional risotto, this is made with pearl barley which is not only very nutritious for your baby but is also delicious. My baby daughter Scarlett adores this.

❋ *From 9 months*

MAKES 4 PORTIONS

1 onion, chopped

1 small red pepper, seeded and chopped

15 ml (1 tbsp) olive oil

175 g (6 oz) pearl barley (well rinsed)

600 ml (1 pint) vegetable stock (see page 35)

50 g (2 oz) brown cap (or button) mushrooms, stalks removed and sliced (optional)

Sauté the onion and red pepper in the oil until softened. Add the barley, stir over a low heat for 2 minutes, then pour over the stock and bring to the boil. Reduce the heat and simmer uncovered, stirring occasionally, for about 35 minutes or until the barley is tender. Add the sliced mushrooms and continue to cook for 6–7 minutes.

# Fairy Toadstools

These toadstools look amazing and they're not difficult to make. For best results, don't put the blobs of mayonnaise on top of the toadstools until the last moment. You could also use thick sticks of cheese for the base of the toadstool and put half a tomato or half a boiled egg on top. Use blobs of tomato ketchup on top of the hard-boiled egg instead of mayonnaise. Watch your child's eyes light up as you bring these to the table!

Level off the top and bottom of the boiled egg so that it stands upright and you can balance half a tomato on top. Using a cream syringe, piping bag or simply the end of a straw, make little blobs of mayonnaise over the surface of the tomato. Place on a bed of salad cress.

*From 9 months*
MAKES 2 PORTIONS
2 hard-boiled eggs, shelled
1 medium tomato
mayonnaise
salad cress

# Chinese Vegetables

Stir-frying is an ideal way to cook because it uses the minimum amount of fat and the vegetables are cooked for only a short amount of time so you keep most of the goodness. Make sure those that need the longest cooking time are put in the pan first.

✳ *From 9 months*

MAKES 5 PORTIONS

30 ml (2 tbsp) vegetable oil

1 small onion, thinly sliced

1 garlic clove, crushed (optional)

175 g (6 oz) broccoli florets

1 medium carrot, cut into strips

15 ml (1 tbsp) water

175 g (6 oz) beansprouts or
  shredded cabbage

50 g (2 oz) baby sweetcorn, cut in
  half lengthways

75 g (3 oz) button mushrooms, sliced

1 medium courgette, cut into strips

50 ml (2 fl oz) chicken stock (see
  page 35)

10 ml ( 2 tsp) light soy sauce

1 large spring onion, chopped

a little freshly ground black pepper

In a wok or large frying pan, heat the oil and sauté the sliced onion and the garlic (if using) until softened. Add the broccoli and carrot, sprinkle with water and cook until slightly softened. Add the shredded cabbage (if using), the sweetcorn, mushrooms and courgette strips. Sauté for 3–4 minutes, then mix in the chicken stock, soy sauce and spring onion. Continue to cook until the vegetables are tender but still crisp (about 5 minutes). If using the beansprouts add at the last minute, and season to taste with pepper. Serve plain, or mixed with Chinese noodles or rice.

# Animal Salad Bowl

*From 9 months*

Make up a bowl of fresh salad ingredients from a selection of the following: different varieties of lettuce, tomato, cucumber, sliced radishes, endive, cooked green beans or sweetcorn, shredded white or red cabbage, hard-boiled eggs, avocado. Toss in your child's favourite salad dressing and top with slices of cheese cut into animal shapes using biscuit cutters. If you don't have any suitable biscuit cutters, cut the cheese into strips instead.

# Cheese and Cherry Tomato Pudding

This has a wonderful soft texture perfect for babies who don't like chewing. It takes only a few minutes to prepare but it's certainly one of my most popular vegetarian dishes and it looks great when it comes out of the oven with a lovely puffed-up, golden topping.

❋ *From 9 months*

MAKES 2 PORTIONS

2 thin slices wholemeal bread

butter or margarine

65 g (2½ oz) mature Cheddar cheese, grated

½ small onion, finely chopped

6 cherry tomatoes, cut in half

2 eggs

175 ml (6 fl oz) whole milk

a pinch of mustard powder

Spread the bread with butter or margarine, and cut each piece into about nine cubes. Grease a small ovenproof dish. Scatter half the bread cubes over the base of the dish and sprinkle over half the cheese, half the onion and half the tomato. Repeat the layers, reserving a little cheese for the top. Beat together the eggs, milk and mustard and pour over the bread cubes. Top with the remaining grated cheese and bake in an oven preheated to 180°C/350°F/Gas 4 for 25–30 minutes or until puffed up and golden.

# Tagliatelle with Broccoli, Mushrooms and Tomato

Combining fresh vegetables with pasta makes a delicious meal for the whole family.

Cook the tagliatelle in a large saucepan of lightly salted water according to the instructions on the packet. When it is ready, drain and toss with a knob of butter.

Steam the broccoli and courgette until tender (4–5 minutes). Melt the butter in a pan and sauté the onion and garlic until softened. Add the mushrooms and sauté for about 3 minutes. Mix a little of the vegetable stock with the cornflour and then stir this back into the remaining stock in a saucepan. Bring to the boil and then stir for one minute until the sauce has thickened. Turn down the heat and stir in the crème fraiche. Remove from the heat and stir in the parmesan cheese. Add the onion, mushrooms, cooked broccoli, courgette and tomato to the sauce and toss this with the tagliatelle.

✳ *From 1 year*

MAKES 4 ADULT PORTIONS

150 g (5 oz) tagliatelle

100 g (4 oz) courgette, cut into matchsticks

100 g (4 oz) broccoli, cut into small florets

25 g (1 oz) butter

1 small onion, finely chopped

1 small clove garlic, crushed

100 g (4 oz) button mushrooms, sliced

250 ml (8 fl oz) vegetable stock

15 ml (1 tbsp) cornflour

60 ml (4 tbsp) crème fraiche

60 g (5 tbsp) parmesan cheese, grated

2 medium tomatoes, skinned, de-seeded and cut into strips

extra parmesan for serving (optional)

# Stuffed Baked Potatoes

Baked potatoes with wonderful tasty ingredients mixed into the cooked flesh make great meals for your child. They are also cheap and easy to prepare.

*From 9 months*

Choose potatoes of roughly the same size and shape so that they will cook in the same length of time. Scrub under cold water, pat dry and prick all over with a fork. Bake for about 1¼ hours or until tender in an oven preheated to 200°C/400°F/Gas 6. To halve the cooking time in a conventional oven, cut the potato in half, score the flesh in lattice fashion, brush with a little melted butter or margarine and place cut side down on a baking tray. Alternatively, scrub and prick potatoes, wrap in absorbent paper and arrange about 2.5 cm (1 inch) apart in a circle and microwave on High (100%), turning over after half the cooking time. The more potatoes you cook at one time, the longer the cooking time. One potato will take about 8 minutes, three or four potatoes will take between 12 and 15 minutes.

Let the potatoes stand for a few minutes before cutting in half. Scoop out the flesh, taking care not to prick the skin. Mash the potato flesh with a little milk and butter and combine with the chosen filling. Try some of these below:

- Fill the hollow with baked beans and top with the creamy mashed potato
- A little sautéed chopped onion with red pepper, sweetcorn and fromage frais topped with grated Cheddar.
- See the recipe ideas on pages 69–71.

# Pizza Potato

Sauté the mushrooms in the butter for 2 minutes, add the tomatoes and oregano and continue to cook for 3 minutes. Cut the potato in half and mash the flesh together with the milk and the 75 g (3 oz) grated cheese. Mix in the tomato and mushrooms and stuff the potatoes. Sprinkle over the grated Cheddar cheese and, if you like, add one of your child's favourite toppings and bake in an oven preheated to 180°C/350°F/Gas 4 for 15–20 minutes.

❉ *From 9 months*
MAKES 4 PORTIONS

2 large potatoes, baked

50 g (2 oz) button mushrooms, sliced

25 g (1 oz) butter or margarine

4 medium tomatoes, skinned, seeded and chopped

a pinch of dried oregano

60 ml (4 tbsp) milk

75 g (3 oz) Mozzarella cheese, grated (or Edam or Cheddar)

25 g (1 oz) Cheddar cheese, grated

# Popeye's Potato

MAKES 2 PORTIONS

1 large potato, baked

100 g (4 oz) fresh or 50 g (2 oz)
  frozen spinach

30 ml (2 tbsp) cream cheese

a little salt and freshly ground
  black pepper (not before 1 year)

20 g (¾ oz) Gruyère cheese, grated

Cook the spinach and finely chop. Mix it together with the cream cheese. Cut the potato in half, mash the flesh, making sure there are no lumps. Mix the mashed potato thoroughly with the creamed spinach. Season lightly and top each half with some grated Gruyère cheese. Heat through in an oven preheated to 180°C/350°F/Gas 4 until the cheese topping is golden, about 15 minutes.

# Potato Men

*From 1 year*
MAKES 4 PORTIONS

2 medium potatoes, baked

50 g (2 oz) Cheddar cheese, grated

3 medium tomatoes, skinned,
  seeded and chopped

1 spring onion, finely chopped
  (optional)

raw carrot sticks for arms and
  legs, peas for eyes, slice of
  tomato or red pepper for the
  mouth

Mash the hot potato flesh with the cheese (reserve a little to sprinkle on top), tomatoes and onion and put back into the potato skins. Heat through and grill until the cheese is bubbling and golden. Allow to cool down a little before serving and decorate with a face, and carrot arms and legs.

# Potato Hedgehogs

Add the ham, cheese and milk to the hot mashed potato and mix together. Refill the hollow skins and fork the top of the mixture to form the prickles of the hedgehog. Grill until golden and decorate with the olives and currants.

*From 1 year*

MAKES 4 PORTIONS

2 medium potatoes, baked

2 slices cooked ham, finely chopped

50 g (2 oz) Cheddar cheese, grated

30 ml (2 tbsp) milk

black olives for the nose and currants for the eyes

# Potato Skins

Much of a potato's goodness is in the skin, and these are delicious served with a special topping like cheese and tomato or cheese and chives or simply with baked beans. They're also great for dipping into tasty dips.

*From 1 year*
MAKES 4 PORTIONS
2 large potatoes (about 225 g/8 oz each)
sunflower oil
some grated Parmesan or Cheddar cheese, chopped tomato or chopped fresh herbs like chives

Scrub the potatoes, rub with a little oil and prick the skin several times with a fork to stop it from bursting. Bake in an oven preheated to 200°C/400°F/Gas 6 for about 1¼ hours or until the flesh is soft. Alternatively, microwave pricked potatoes on High for 12–15 minutes depending on size. They will crisp up when they are baked in the oven later. Let cool, then cut in half and scoop out most of the flesh (you can make this into mashed potato and freeze it) but leave about 5 mm (¼ inch) flesh around the inside of the skin. Cut the skins lengthways into about 3 strips, brush on both sides with oil then return to the oven and bake for about 15 minutes or until crisp. Top with some grated cheese, tomato and herbs or Greek yoghurt, mixed with grated carrot and topped with grated Cheddar, and cook under a preheated grill for about 5 minutes. Alternatively, season lightly, bake in the oven and serve with a tasty dip like a guacamole: blend avocado with a little grated onion, chopped tomato, a squeeze of lemon juice and cream cheese or simply mix together cream cheese, cottage cheese, snipped chives and a little ketchup or a dash of Worcestershire sauce.

# Sunflower Supper Surprise

As cookery writer for *Maternity and Mothercraft*, the oldest established baby magazine in this country, I ran a competition to design a healthy, cheap, fun meal for a young child. This recipe, sent in by an NNEB student, was one of the prizewinners.

Beat together the eggs, milk and cheese. Place in a pan with a knob of butter, and scramble. Toast the bread and spread lightly with butter. Remove the crusts, cut into small triangles, and place around the sides of the plate. Heap the scrambled egg into the centre of the plate and arrange a circle of tomato halves around the edge. Cut a piece of the cucumber into a long strip to represent a stalk, and add a small lettuce leaf at either side.

*From 1 year*

MAKES 1 PORTION

2 eggs

25 ml (1 fl oz) milk

25 g (1 oz) Cheddar or Gruyère cheese, grated

butter

2 slices wholemeal bread

4 or 5 cherry tomatoes, cut in half

slice of cucumber and lettuce for garnish

# Simple Simon's Scrambled Egg

*From 1 year*
MAKES 2 PORTIONS

1 medium tomato, skinned, de-
    seeded and chopped

15 g (½ oz) butter

2 eggs, lightly beaten

30 ml (2 tbsp) milk

a knob of butter

22.5 ml (1½ tbsp) grated Gruyère
    cheese

Beat the eggs together with the milk and season lightly. Melt the butter in a small saucepan, add the chopped tomato and sauté over a low heat for one minute. Add the egg mixture and heat, stirring continuously with a wooden spoon until the eggs start to cook. Add the cheese and continue to cook until the eggs are set. Serve immediately.

# Nuts about Nuts!

Nuts are probably not very popular with most children. However, this is a really tasty recipe and your child won't know it's made with nuts unless you tell him! Serve plain or with sauce. This is not suitable for children under the age of two.

Sauté the onion in the butter until soft, then add the mushrooms and sauté for 3–4 minutes. Meanwhile chop the cashew nuts in a food processor and mix them together with the wholemeal breadcrumbs. Add the nut mix to the onion and mushrooms and stir in the stock. Form the mixture into 15 walnut-sized balls, roll in breadcrumbs and sauté in vegetable oil until golden.

Pour the sauce over the cashew nut balls, heat through and serve.

**N** ✳ *From 2 years*

MAKES 15 BALLS

1 medium onion, finely chopped

25 g (1 oz) butter

175 g (6 oz) brown cap (or button) mushrooms, chopped

175 g (6 oz) cashew nuts

75 g (3 oz) wholemeal breadcrumbs

50 ml (2 fl oz) vegetable stock (see page 35)

fine breadcrumbs

vegetable oil

½ quantity home-made tomato sauce (see page 114)

# Rice, Vegetable and Cashew Nut Slices

This is good served on its own, hot or cold, or with the tomato sauce on page 114. You can double the quantity of this recipe to make a delicious family meal. Do not serve to children under two years because of the nuts.

**N** *From 2 years*

MAKES 5 SLICES

75 g (3 oz) basmati or brown rice, rinsed in a sieve under the cold tap

1 small onion, finely chopped

1 medium carrot, grated

15 g (½ oz) butter or margarine

50 g (2 oz) mushrooms, finely chopped

50 g (2 oz) wholemeal breadcrumbs

50 g (2 oz) cashew nuts, finely chopped in a food processor

50 g (2 oz) Cheddar cheese, grated

1 egg, lightly beaten

Cook the rice according to the packet instructions. Meanwhile sauté the onion and carrot in the butter for about 5 minutes, stirring occasionally. Add the mushrooms and continue to cook for a further 5 minutes. Remove from the heat and mix the vegetables together with the cooked rice, breadcrumbs, chopped nuts, grated cheese and egg. Grease a small (450 g/1 lb) loaf tin, spoon the mixture into the tin, flatten the top and bake for about 45 minutes in an oven preheated to 180°C/350°F/Gas 4. Cut into slices and serve.

# Favourite Fish Recipes

Fish is a wonderful food for growing children; it's a good source of protein, vitamins and minerals, and quick and easy to cook. If your child's idea of fish is a plate of fish fingers, let him sample some of the tasty ways with fish in this section – like Spiky Fish Cakes, Fish Florentina or Sweet and Sour Fish.
*Always watch out for bones when giving fish to children.*

Below are five different methods of cooking 225 g (8 oz) fish fillet. Take care not to overcook fish; it's ready when it flakes easily with a fork. If you wish, you can lightly season the fish prior to cooking, for babies over one year only.

*To microwave,* place the fish in a suitable dish, sprinkle with water, milk or a little lemon juice and dot with butter or margarine. Cover and microwave, on full power, for 3–4 minutes.

*To bake in an oven,* place the fish in a greased casserole, squeeze over a few drops of lemon juice and dot with butter or margarine then cover with foil. Bake in an oven preheated to 180°C/350°F/Gas 4 for 10–12 minutes.

*To steam,* put the fish on a plate, add 1 tablespoon milk and dot with a little butter. Place on top of a saucepan of boiling water, cover with another plate and cook for about 12 minutes.

*To grill,* lay the fish on a greased grill pan or foil, dot with butter or margarine, squeeze over a few drops of lemon juice, and grill for about 3–4 minutes on each side.

*To sauté,* dip the fish fillet in seasoned flour and fry in butter or margarine for 4–5 minutes, turning halfway through.

# Fish in a Blanket

This tempting golden fillet of fish is really easy to make.
Serve with grilled tomatoes, which you can cook alongside
the fish, and mashed potato. Add extra milk and leave out
the seasoning for young babies.

*From 6 months*

MAKES 2 PORTIONS

1 x 225 g (8 oz) fillet white fish,
   skinned (cod, haddock or hake)

a little salt and freshly ground
   black pepper (not before 1 year)

20 g (¾ oz) butter

25 g (1 oz) Gruyère, Edam or
   Cheddar cheese, finely grated

10 ml (2 tsp) milk

Season the fish with a little salt and pepper, dot with half
the butter and grill on one side only for 3–4 minutes.
Meanwhile, to make the topping, cream together the
remaining butter, cheese and milk in a small bowl. Turn the
fish over, spread the topping on the uncooked side and grill
for 6–8 minutes or until the fish flakes easily with a fork.

# Braised Fish with Potato

## A tasty, easy-to-prepare recipe which is very popular.

Sauté the onion and pepper in the oil until soft. Add the tomato, potato and rosemary (if used), and pour over 120 ml (4 fl oz) of the stock. Simmer for 15–20 minutes or until the potato is tender. Lay the fish fillet over the cooked potatoes, pour over the remaining stock, cover and simmer for about 10 minutes or until the fish flakes easily with a fork. Remove the rosemary, then flake the fish, mix together with the potato and serve. For young babies, mash the potato and fish together.

❋ *From 7 months*

MAKES 3 PORTIONS

½ small onion, chopped

1 small red pepper, chopped

15 ml (1 tbsp) vegetable oil

1 medium tomato, skinned, seeded and chopped

1 medium potato (about 150 g/ 5 oz), peeled and diced

a tiny sprig fresh rosemary (optional)

175 ml (6 fl oz) chicken or vegetable stock (see page 34 or 35)

175 g (6 oz) fillet of cod, skinned

# Saucy Cod

A delicious fish dish, excellent for young babies.
Serve with creamy mashed potatoes.

✻ *From 8 months*

MAKES 3 PORTIONS

½ onion, chopped

30 g (1 oz) butter

15 ml (1 tbsp) vegetable oil

1 courgette, sliced

300 g (12 oz) tomatoes, skinned,
   seeded and cut into chunks

15 ml (1 tbsp) tomato purée

225 g (8 oz) fillet of cod,
   haddock or hake, skinned

a squeeze of lemon juice

a little salt and freshly ground
   black pepper (not before 1 year)

Sauté the onion in 15 g (½ oz) of the butter and the oil until softened. Add the courgette, tomato and tomato purée and simmer, stirring occasionally, for about 10 minutes. Meanwhile, put the fish into an ovenproof dish, dot with tiny knobs of butter and sprinkle with lemon juice, and season lightly. Bake in the oven (see page 77) until cooked through and the flesh flakes easily. Purée the vegetables in a mouli to make a smooth sauce. Flake the fish, making sure there are no bones, pour the sauce over and serve with mashed potatoes.

# Haddock with a Tomato, Cheese and Herb Crust

Sometimes children aren't too keen on eating plain grilled fish, so I've come up with this appetising topping. You can try using all sorts of herbs like basil, tarragon, chives or mixed dried herbs. For young babies, flake the fish carefully, checking to make sure there are no bones.

Lightly season the fish, dot with margarine, and grill for 4 minutes on each side under a preheated grill. Mix together the Parmesan, parsley and breadcrumbs. When the fish is cooked, cover with the chopped tomatoes and sprinkle the breadcrumb mixture over. Place under a preheated grill for about 3 minutes.

*From 9 months*

MAKES 2–3 PORTIONS

2 x 175 g (6 oz) fillets of haddock (or cod, hake, or turbot)

a little salt and freshly ground black pepper (not before 1 year)

25 g (1 oz) margarine

1 tablespoon Parmesan cheese, grated

a pinch of parsley, chopped

1½ tablespoons breadcrumbs

100 g (4 oz) tomatoes (about 2 medium), skinned, seeded and chopped

# Sweet and Sour Fish

This makes a very tasty fish dish and is good served on a bed of fluffy white rice. Flake the fish and mix with the rice for small children. Always take care to check that there are no bones in the fish.

☀ *From 1 year*

MAKES 4 PORTIONS

300 g (10 oz) fillet of cod, skinned and cut into cubes, or 300 g (10 oz) lemon or Dover sole fillets, skinned and cut into strips

seasoned plain flour

22.5 ml (1½ tbsp) vegetable oil

SWEET AND SOUR SAUCE

15 ml (1 tbsp) white wine vinegar

15 ml (1 tbsp) sugar

22.5 ml (1½ tbsp) tomato ketchup

7.5 ml (½ tbsp) soy sauce

7.5 ml (½ tbsp) cornflour

45 ml (3 tbsp) water

2.5 ml (½ tsp) sesame oil

15 ml (1 tbsp) finely sliced spring onion

Coat the fish in seasoned flour and sauté in the oil for 4–5 minutes or until cooked (it should flake easily with a fork). Mix together the ingredients for the sauce and heat gently in a saucepan, stirring until thickened. Pour the sauce over the fish and heat through.

# Yummy Fish in Orange Sauce

This is a delicious combination of flavours, one of my children's favourites, and it takes just a few minutes to cook.

Melt the butter or margarine in a frying pan and sauté the fish for about 6 minutes, turning occasionally. Add the soy sauce, turn the heat up and bring to the boil. Cook for about 1 minute. Pour in the orange juice and cook until the sauce has slightly reduced. Take the fish off the bone, flake the fish carefully, making sure there are no stray bones, and mix with the orange sauce.

✳ *From 9 months*
MAKES 1–2 PORTIONS
20 g (¾ oz) butter or margarine
1 x 225 g (8 oz) cutlet of cod, hake, haddock or halibut, on the bone
7.5 ml (1½ tsp) light soy sauce
45 ml (3 tbsp) freshly squeezed orange juice

# Fish Florentina

Fillets of fish on a bed of spinach and covered with a cheese sauce is a classic combination which babies love too. For young babies, simply mash all the ingredients together with a fork.

✳ *From 9 months*

MAKES 6 PORTIONS

300 g (10 oz) cod fillet, skinned (or use haddock, hake or plaice)

a knob of butter

30 ml (2 tbsp) milk

175 g (6 oz) fresh spinach, carefully washed and tough stalks removed, or 75 g (3 oz) frozen spinach

CHEESE SAUCE

25 g (1 oz) butter

25 g (1 oz) flour

300 ml (½ pint) milk

a pinch of grated nutmeg (optional)

25 g (1 oz) Gruyère cheese, grated

25 g (1 oz) Cheddar cheese, grated

Put the fish in a suitable dish, dot with the butter and add the milk. Cover, leaving an air vent, and cook on high for 3½ to 4 minutes or until the fish is properly cooked through. Alternatively you could poach the fish in a saucepan with the milk for the sauce and then strain the cooking liquid from the fish and use this to make the cheese sauce with.

Cook the spinach in a covered saucepan for 3–4 minutes or until tender. After washing there will be enough water clinging to the leaves so you won't need to add any more. If you are using frozen spinach, follow the cooking instructions. Press out any excess liquid from the spinach and roughly chop it.

To make the cheese sauce, melt the butter, stir in the flour and cook gently for about 1 minute. Gradually whisk in the milk. Remove from the heat and stir in the grated cheeses and nutmeg (if using).

Flake the cooked fish. Arrange the spinach in a dish or use several small dishes, cover with a layer of flaked fish and top with the cheese sauce. You can sprinkle with a little extra grated cheese and brown the top under a preheated grill if you wish.

# Chinese-style Fish with Carrots and Baby Sweetcorn

A good introduction to the delights of Chinese cooking. Children love fish cooked this way as it has a wonderful flavour and it's soft and moist. Flake the fish for young children. This is good served with rice.

In a saucepan, mix together all the ingredients for the sauce apart from the spring onions. Bring to the boil and then simmer, stirring, for 2–3 minutes until thickened and smooth. Stir in the spring onion.

Heat half the vegetable oil and a knob of butter in a frying pan. Coat the fish in seasoned flour and sauté the fish for 2–3 minutes on each side or until cooked. Heat the remaining oil in a pan and sauté the vegetables for about 3 minutes or until tender. Add the vegetables to the fish, pour over the sauce and heat through.

*From 1 year*

MAKES 6 PORTIONS

30 ml (2 tbsp) vegetable oil

a knob of butter

350 g (12 oz) plaice, sole or cod fillets, skinned and cut into strips

seasoned flour

50 g (2 oz) baby corn, quartered lengthways

50 g (2 oz) courgette, cut into strips

50 g (2 oz) carrot, cut into strips

SAUCE

250 ml (8 fl oz) chicken stock

10 ml (2 tsp) soy sauce

5 ml (1 tsp) sesame oil

15 ml (1 tbsp) sugar

5 ml (1 tsp) cider vinegar

15 ml (1 tbsp) cornflour

1 spring onion, finely sliced

# Ley's Fish Pie

Ley is a friend of mine who runs cookery courses from her home, and this is one of her favourite fish recipes.

❋ *From 1 year*

MAKES 4 PORTIONS

550 g (1¼ lb) potatoes, peeled
   and cut into chunks

175 g (6 oz) salmon fillet, skinned

175 g (6 oz) cod fillet (or haddock,
   lemon sole or hake), skinned

seasoned plain flour

70 g (2¾ oz) butter or margarine

½ onion, thinly sliced

175 g (6 oz) brown cap (or button)
   mushrooms, stalks removed and
   sliced

350 g (12 oz) ripe tomatoes,
   skinned and sliced

a handful of parsley, dill
   or chives, chopped

a little salt and freshly ground
   black pepper

30 ml (2 tbsp) milk

1 egg yolk, beaten with 15 ml
   (1 tbsp) water

Boil the potatoes until soft. Cut the fish into chunks, dip in seasoned flour and fry in 25 g (1 oz) of the butter until just cooked. Drain well and set aside. Fry the onions in 25 g (1 oz) more of the butter until soft and golden, about 10 minutes. Add the tomatoes and cook for 2–3 minutes. Add the mushrooms and cook for 3–4 minutes. Mix in the fresh herbs and some seasoning. Mash the potatoes with the milk and remaining butter, making sure there are no lumps, then season to taste. In an ovenproof dish or several small dishes place a layer of vegetables at the bottom, cover with a layer of fish and repeat these two layers again, finishing with the vegetables. Cover with the mashed potatoes and brush with the beaten water and egg yolk. Bake in an oven preheated to 180°C/350°F/Gas 4 for about 35 minutes.

# Nicholas's Spiky Fish Cakes

Fish cakes have been good nursery fare for many years, but sometimes they can be quite bland. These fish cakes have a delicious crispy potato coating and the peas and sweetcorn add a sweet flavour. Children like them much better than ordinary fish cakes!

Chop the fish by hand or coarsely with short bursts in a food processor. Mix in the spring onion, parsley, frozen peas and sweetcorn, and season with salt and pepper. Add enough beaten egg to bind the mixture. Squeeze the excess water out of the potatoes and season them with a little salt and pepper. Form the fish into eight to ten walnut-sized balls using your hands and roll in the grated potato to make a fairly thick coating (I like lots of potato because it makes them lovely and crispy). Slightly flatten the balls and fry in a mixture of oil and butter until crispy and golden. Drain well on kitchen paper before serving.

❄ *From 1 year*

MAKES 8–10 BALLS

225 g (8 oz) fish, filleted and skinned (haddock, cod, hake or salmon)

2 tablespoons spring onions, finely chopped

a handful of parsley, chopped

40 g (1½ oz) frozen peas

40 g (1½ oz) frozen sweetcorn

a little salt and freshly ground pepper

½ lightly beaten egg

2 large potatoes, peeled and roughly grated

15 ml (1 tbsp) vegetable oil

15 g (½ oz) butter or margarine

# Chicken at its Best

We all love chicken in our family, and it's so versatile, from a good old-fashioned roast chicken to sticky drumsticks and oven-barbecued chicken. Here are some family favourites for you to try.

# Two-way Chicken

This works well for babies, finely chopped, or serve on a bed of rice for older children. It also makes a tasty pasta sauce and as a variation you could leave out the chicken and add 50 g (2 oz) steamed broccoli florets or 50 g (2 oz) frozen peas.

Put the chicken stock, onion, parsley and peppercorns into a saucepan. Add the chicken, bring to the boil and let simmer for about 8 minutes or until the chicken is cooked through. Remove the chicken and finely chop. Meanwhile sauté the mushrooms in the margarine for 2–3 minutes. Stir in the flour to make a paste, then gradually stir in the milk until the sauce has thickened. Remove from the heat and stir in the grated cheese. Add the chopped chicken. Roughly purée the sauce in a blender for young babies and add a little extra milk if necessary.

✳ *From 9 months*

MAKES 3 PORTIONS

175 ml (6 fl oz) weak chicken
   stock (see page 34)

1 small piece of onion

1 sprig fresh parsley

a few black peppercorns

1 small boneless chicken breast,
   cut into chunks

25 g (1 oz) margarine or butter

50 g (2 oz) mushrooms, washed
   and sliced

12.5 g (½ oz) plain flour

250 ml (8 fl oz) milk

25 g (1 oz) Gruyère cheese, grated

# Cheesy Chicken and Broccoli

A very tasty chicken dish that could also be made with
leftover cooked chicken. Chop into small pieces or leave out the pasta
and purée for young babies.

✳ *From 9 months*
MAKES 4 PORTIONS

1 chicken breast, skinned
  (about 150 g/5 oz)
15 ml (1 tbsp) vegetable oil
300 ml (½ pint) chicken stock
  (see page 34)
60 g (2½ oz) pasta (optional)
65 g (2½ oz) broccoli, cut into
  small florets
1 quantity home-made cheese
  sauce made with 25 g (1 oz)
  grated Cheddar and 25 g (1 oz)
  grated Gruyère (see page 84)
a pinch of mustard powder
  (optional)
1 egg yolk

Cut the chicken breast into bite-sized pieces, and either
sauté in the vegetable oil or poach in the chicken stock
until cooked through. Cook the pasta according to the
instructions on the packet if using. Steam or boil the broccoli
until tender (about 6 minutes) and set aside. When preparing
the cheese sauce, stir in the mustard (if using) instead of
nutmeg. Mix together the chicken, broccoli, pasta and half
the cheese sauce and place in an ovenproof dish (or two small
dishes). Beat the egg yolk into the rest of the cheese sauce and
pour on top. Bake in an oven preheated to 180°C/350°F/Gas
4 for 20 minutes.

# Mrs Rabbit's Chicken Slices

A lovely and moist simple-to-prepare chicken loaf, packed with Vitamin A. You could also use this chicken and carrot mixture to make chicken burgers.

C hop the chicken meat in a food processor and mix with the rest of the ingredients. Spoon the mixture into a small loaf tin and cook for 30 minutes in an oven preheated to 180°C/350°F/Gas 4. Serve in slices, or mash for young babies.

❊ *From 9 months*
MAKES 4 PORTIONS
the meat from 4 chicken thighs
    (about 225 g/8 oz)
2 carrots, scrubbed and grated
    (about 110 g/4 oz)
1 small onion, grated
50 g (2 oz) wholemeal
    breadcrumbs
1 egg, lightly beaten
18 g (1 heaped tbsp) parsley,
    chopped
a little salt and freshly ground
    black pepper (not before 1 year)
15 ml (1 tbsp) tomato ketchup

# Chicken Balls with Tomato Sauce and Pasta

This is a good recipe for encouraging pasta fans to eat more chicken.

❇ *From 9 months*

MAKES 15 CHICKEN BALLS

2 chicken breasts (about 275 g/10 oz), skinned and finely chopped for a few seconds in a food processor

½ small onion, finely chopped

a handful of parsley, chopped

2 tablespoons breadcrumbs

1 small apple, peeled and finely grated (squeeze to get rid of some of the liquid)

½ beaten egg

15 ml (1 tbsp) vegetable oil

SAUCE

½ quantity home-made tomato sauce (see page 114)

1 medium carrot, finely chopped

100 g (4 oz) bow-tie pasta

Mix all the ingredients for the chicken balls together, except for the oil, then using wet hands, form into about fifteen walnut-sized balls. Fry the balls in shallow oil until golden, then drain well.

When preparing the sauce, sauté the carrot with the onion, then continue as on page 114. If your child likes a smooth sauce, you may want to blend it. Add the chicken balls and simmer in the sauce for 6–8 minutes. Meanwhile, cook the pasta according to the directions on the packet. Mix the chicken balls together with the pasta.

# Mango Chicken Risotto

This rice has a lovely flavour and can also be served without the mango. However, if your child likes the combination of chicken and mango, another good, easy recipe is to mix bite-sized pieces of cooked chicken with cooked pasta, pour over a light vinaigrette and add some chopped-up pieces of mango.

Sauté the onion in the butter until softened, then add the rice and stir until well coated. Stir in the curry powder then pour over the chicken stock and add the cinnamon stick. Cover and simmer for 25–30 minutes or until the rice is tender. Meanwhile sauté the chicken in the oil until cooked through, about 6–8 minutes, and then chop into bite-sized pieces. Remove the cinnamon stick, combine the cooked rice with the chicken and mango and serve hot or cold.

*From 9 months*
MAKES 5 PORTIONS
½ onion, finely chopped
15 g (½ oz) butter
225 g (8 oz) basmati rice, rinsed in a sieve under the cold tap
2.5 ml (½ tsp) mild curry powder
600 ml (1 pint) chicken stock (see page 34)
1 cinnamon stick
1 large or 2 small boneless chicken breasts, skinned (about 200 g/7 oz)
15 ml (1 tbsp) vegetable oil
¼ ripe mango, peeled and chopped

# Rice 'n' Easy

This lovely oven-baked rice dish is always popular. For vegetarians you could leave out the chopped chicken and use vegetable stock.

❋ *From 9 months*

MAKES 4 ADULT PORTIONS

30 ml (2 tbsp) olive oil

1 large banana shallot or 1 small onion, chopped

½ small red pepper, de-seeded and chopped

15 ml (1 tbsp) chopped parsley

225 g (8 oz) chicken breast, chopped

450 ml (¾ pint) passata

1 chicken stock cube dissolved in 100 ml (3½ fl oz) boiling water

15 ml (1 tbsp) garlic purée

5 ml (1 tsp) caster sugar

salt and pepper

200 g (7 oz) long grain white rice

Heat the oil in a large saucepan and sauté the shallot, red pepper and parsley for about 5 minutes. Add the chopped chicken and sauté stirring occasionally, until it turns opaque. Add the passata, the chicken stock, garlic purée and sugar and season with salt and pepper. Cook, uncovered, for 15 minutes. Meanwhile, cook the rice according to the packet instructions. Drain the rice when cooked and mix with the tomato sauce.

# Chicken and Mushroom Burgers

*Chicken breasts can sometimes be quite dry, so I make these burgers using chicken thighs which are lovely and moist.*

Skin the chicken, take the flesh off the bone, and remove and discard any fat. You should have about 225 g (8 oz) meat. Chop for a few seconds in a food processor. Meanwhile, sauté the onion and mushrooms in the margarine for about 4 minutes. Combine the chicken, onion and mushrooms, breadcrumbs, Worcestershire sauce (if using), and season lightly. Shape the mixture into about four small burgers, dip in beaten egg and coat in flour. Fry in shallow oil until golden and cooked through, about 5 minutes. Alternatively, brush with a little oil and cook under a preheated grill, turning halfway through the cooking time.

❋ *From 1 year*

MAKES 4 BURGERS

4 chicken thighs

½ large onion, chopped

40 g (1½ oz) brown cap (or button) mushrooms, chopped

40 g (1½ oz) margarine

25 g (1 oz) breadcrumbs

a few drops of Worcestershire sauce (optional)

a little salt and freshly ground black pepper

1 egg, beaten

plain flour

vegetable oil

# Raymonde's Easy Drumsticks

My friend Raymonde is a busy working mother with twins, so she's always looking for quick and easy recipes she can make when she gets home from work. This is simplicity itself but looks and tastes wonderful. Serve with a baked potato and some baked beans or salad – it's probably best to take the chicken off the bone for children under three.

*From 1 year*
MAKES 2 PORTIONS

2 large chicken drumsticks

MARINADE 1

15 ml (1 tbsp) tomato ketchup

15 ml (1 tbsp) runny honey

5 ml (1 tsp) vegetable oil

a few drops of Worcestershire
    sauce

a pinch of paprika

MARINADE 2

15 ml (1 tbsp) runny honey

15 ml (1 tbsp) soy sauce (or lemon
    juice)

a knob of butter or margarine

In a saucepan, gently heat the ingredients for the marinade chosen. Make two fairly deep cuts in the drumsticks (remove the skin if your child prefers), and leave to marinate in the chosen marinade for an hour or longer. Put the drumsticks in a small ovenproof dish on a sheet of foil with the edges turned up and cook under a preheated grill for about 25 minutes, or until cooked through. Baste occasionally with the juices and turn frequently so that all sides are cooked. Alternatively, bake in an oven preheated to 180°C/350°F/Gas 4 for about 35 minutes or until cooked through, turning and basting occasionally.

# Chicken Chow Mein

Serve with Chinese noodles which you can cook in chicken stock or, if your child prefers, serve with basmati rice. To save time you could use a ready-prepared selection of stir-fry vegetables.

S kin the boned chicken breasts and cut into strips. Mix together the marinade ingredients, and marinate the chicken strips for at least an hour. Chop the onion and sauté in vegetable or sesame oil in a wok or frying pan until softened. Cut the carrot into strips and stir-fry for 4–5 minutes. Add the chicken and fry until just cooked. Add the mushrooms, courgette (cut into strips) and baby sweetcorn, and stir-fry for 2–3 minutes. Mix together the ingredients for the sauce, pour this over the vegetables and cook the vegetables until tender, taking care not to overcook them, and adding the beansprouts at the last minute.

❊ *From 1 year*

MAKES 4 PORTIONS

2 chicken breasts

1 small onion

30 ml (2 tbsp) oil

1 medium carrot

50 g (2 oz) mushrooms, sliced

1 medium courgette

75 g (3 oz) baby sweetcorn, halved
   lengthways

100 g (4 oz) beansprouts

MARINADE

15 ml (1 tbsp) light soy sauce

15 ml (1 tbsp) egg white (optional)

5 ml (1 tsp) sesame oil

1 teaspoon cornflour

SAUCE

120 ml (4 fl oz) chicken stock (see
   page 34)

15 ml (1 tbsp) apple juice

15 ml (1 tbsp) light soy sauce

1 teaspoon cornflour

# Chicken with Matchsticks

As a special treat, my children love to eat this using chopsticks. It's very easy to make them user friendly for a three year old: simply roll up a piece of paper and secure it with a rubber band between the chopsticks at the top. It should then be simple for a child to pick up food by pinching the chopsticks together with his thumb and two fingers.

❋ *From 1 year*
MAKES 2–3 PORTIONS
2 chicken breasts
a little salt and freshly ground
  black pepper
22.5 ml (1½ tbsp) vegetable oil
40 g (1½ oz) carrot matchsticks
40 g (1½ oz) courgette
  matchsticks (unpeeled)
40 g (1½ oz) baby sweetcorns,
  sliced in half lengthways
SAUCE
5 ml (1 tsp) red wine vinegar
15 ml (1 tbsp) sauce
15 ml (1 tbsp) tomato ketchup
15 ml (1 tbsp) olive oil
30 ml (2 tbsp) pineapple juice
5 ml (1 tsp) sugar

Mix all the ingredients for the sauce together and set aside. Skin the boned chicken breasts and cut into strips. Season them with a little salt and pepper and sauté for 4–5 minutes or until cooked through. Drain on kitchen paper. Steam the carrot, courgette and baby sweetcorn for about 4 minutes so that they are cooked but still crunchy. Bring the sauce to the boil, simmer for about a minute and stir in the vegetable strips and chicken.

# Oven-barbecued Chicken

This chicken has the most wonderful taste without any of the bother of lighting a barbecue. I've yet to find a child who doesn't like it!

Sauté the onion in the oil until soft, then add the remaining ingredients apart from the chicken. Simmer for 3–4 minutes. Trim the excess fat from the chicken, and cut two deep slits in each of the breasts. Place the breasts in an ovenproof dish and coat with the sauce. Cover with foil and bake in an oven preheated to 180°C/350°F/Gas 4 for 30 minutes, occasionally basting with the sauce. Remove the foil and continue to cook for 10 minutes. Take off the bone, cut into pieces and mix with the sauce.

*Note*: if you would like more sauce with the chicken, simply double the quantity.

✳ *From 1 year*

MAKES 4 PORTIONS

½ onion, chopped

15 ml (1 tbsp) vegetable oil

1 garlic clove, crushed (optional)

45 ml (3 tbsp) tomato ketchup

7.5 ml (1½ tsp) lemon juice

5 ml (1 tsp) light soy sauce

5 ml (1 tsp) Worcestershire sauce

45 ml (3 tbsp) water

2 chicken breasts on the bone, skinned

# Yum Yum Chicken

Everyone in the family loves this, even my baby Scarlett who likes the chicken in strips so that she can pick them up with her fingers and dip them in the sauce. It's very simple so it's a good dish for when the children have friends over for tea, served with some green vegetables.

❋ *From 1 year*

MAKES 2–4 PORTIONS

2 chicken breasts off the bone, skinned

a little salt and freshly ground black pepper

a pinch of dried herbs

½ small onion, peeled

20 g (¾ oz) butter or margarine

75 g (3 oz) button mushrooms, sliced

1 x 225 g (8 oz) can of chopped tomatoes

2.5 ml (½ tsp) dried oregano

40 g (1½ oz) Gruyère cheese, grated (optional)

Season the chicken and sprinkle with some mixed herbs. Place in an ovenproof dish. Sauté the onion in the butter until soft, then add the mushrooms and sauté for 2–3 minutes more. Add the chopped tomatoes, sprinkle over the oregano and simmer for about 12 minutes. Pour the tomato and mushroom sauce over the chicken breasts and top with grated cheese if used. Bake in an oven preheated to180°C/350°F/Gas 4 for about 25 minutes.

# Making the Most of Meat

Iron deficiency is the most common nutritional problem in the world today. With red meat being the best source of iron, I have tried to create some tasty, tempting meaty recipes to ensure that your child gets sufficient iron in his or her diet. Many mothers are turning away from red meat in favour of fish and chicken but if young children don't have enough iron in their diet, they become anaemic.

Liver is probably the richest source of iron for your child and it's soft to chew and easy to digest. Grill it or dip thin slices in seasoned flour, shaking off the excess and sauté in butter or margarine until cooked but still slightly pink in the centre (about one minute each side). You can add flavour by mixing with sautéed onion, mushroom or tomato, some sage or perhaps adding a little orange juice towards the end of the cooking time. Serve with mashed potato or rice.

# Marina's Tempting Twirls

This is really tasty recipe for all the family and if, like me, you have a baby who is a reluctant meat-eater but who loves pasta, then this is a good recipe to try. Red meat is the best form of iron and you can disguise the fact that there is meat in the sauce by blending it in a food processor for a couple of seconds. Hopefully, your baby will be so happy to see her favourite pasta she'll eat it all up!

✳ *From 9 months*
MAKES 6 PORTIONS
½ onion, chopped
15 ml (1 tbsp) vegetable oil
225 g (8 oz) lean minced beef
a few drops Worcestershire sauce
  (optional)
½ quantity home-made tomato
  sauce (see page 114)
½ red pepper, cored, seeded and
  chopped
225 g (8 oz) three-colour fusilli (or
  pasta bows or shells)
3 tablespoons Parmesan cheese,
  grated (optional)

Sauté the onion in the oil until softened but not coloured, then add the meat and cook until browned. Stir in a few drops of Worcestershire sauce and set aside. When making the tomato sauce, sauté the pepper with the onion, then continue as on page 114. After 10 minutes' simmering, stir in the meat and continue to simmer for 6–8 minutes more. Transfer the meat in tomato sauce to a food processor and chop for 3–4 seconds. Cook the pasta according to the instructions on the packet and mix the meat in tomato sauce together with the cooked pasta. Sprinkle with Parmesan cheese, if using.

# Mini Meatballs in a Tasty Sauce

The dainty size of these meatballs is very appealing to children and they're good with rice or mashed potatoes to mop up the sauce. I use challah, a plaited white loaf, to make the breadcrumbs as it gives the meatballs a particularly nice taste.

Mix the meat with the breadcrumbs, seasoning, egg, onion and parsley. Using your hands, form into about 24 small meatballs, then sauté in shallow oil until browned. Remove the meatballs and drain well. For the sauce, fry the onion in the oil until softened. Stir in the flour to make a paste and then stir in the stock, tomato purée and soy sauce. Bring to the boil and simmer for a few minutes. Place the meatballs in a small casserole dish, cover with the sauce, and cook in an oven preheated to 160°C/325°F/Gas 3 for 45–50 minutes. About 20 minutes before the end, add the sliced mushrooms.

❋ *From 1 year*

MAKES 24 MEATBALLS

450 g (1 lb) lean minced beef

75 g (3 oz) fresh white breadcrumbs

a little salt and freshly ground black pepper

1 egg, beaten

½ onion, finely chopped

a handful of parsley, chopped

sunflower oil

SAUCE

1 onion, thinly sliced

7.5 ml (½ tbsp) sunflower oil

1 tablespoon plain flour

450 ml (¾ pint) good beef stock

30 ml (2 tbsp) tomato purée

15 ml (1 tbsp) soy sauce

75 g (3 oz) brown cap (or button) mushrooms, sliced

# Smiley Faces

I freeze these in individual small round containers and decorate the faces just before serving.

✳ *From 1 year*

MAKES 4 SMILEY FACES

450 g (1 lb) potatoes, peeled and
   cut into chunks

25 g (1 oz) butter or margarine

30 ml (2 tbsp) milk

a little salt and freshly ground
   black pepper

1 small onion, grated

225 g (8 oz) lean minced beef

15 ml (1 tbsp) vegetable oil

½ chicken stock cube, dissolved
   in 120 ml (4 fl oz) water

1 x 150 g (5 oz) can of baked
   beans

grated cheese for the hair, peas
   for the eyes, carrot for the nose,
   tomato or red pepper for the
   mouth

Boil the potatoes until soft, then mash together with the butter and milk. Season lightly. Meanwhile, sauté the onion and beef in the oil until browned, then chop for a couple of seconds in a food processor. Add the chicken stock, and simmer for 10 minutes. Transfer the meat to individual dishes and cover with a layer of baked beans and then the mashed potato. Dot with a little butter or margarine, heat through and brown under the grill for a few minutes. Add the eyes, nose, mouth and hair.

# Cheesy Stuffed Peppers

A really tasty recipe and if your children don't like peppers, serve the meat and rice in a dish on its own.

Cut the peppers in half and carefully remove seeds and membrane. Cover with boiling water and simmer for 2 minutes, rinse under cold water and drain. Cook the rice according to the instructions on the packet. Sauté the onion, garlic (if using) and parsley in the oil until softened. Add the mince, stirring until browned. Chop the meat and onion for a couple of seconds in a food processor. Return to the pan and add the chopped tomatoes and their juices, the tomato purée and seasoning. Bring to the boil and simmer, uncovered, for 20–25 minutes. Mix in the rice and grated Mozzarella cheese. Fill the pepper halves with the cheesy beef mixture, place in a greased ovenproof dish, cover with foil and bake in an oven preheated to 180°C/350°F/Gas 4 for 35–40 minutes.

✳ *From 1 year*

MAKES 4 PORTIONS

2 large peppers, red, green or
    yellow

65 g (2½ oz) basmati rice, rinsed
    in a sieve under the cold tap

1 small onion, finely chopped

1 garlic clove, crushed (optional)

a handful of parsley, chopped

15 ml (1 tbsp) vegetable oil

225 g (8 oz) lean minced beef

1 x 400 g (14 oz) can of chopped
    tomatoes

30 ml (2 tbsp) tomato purée

a little salt and freshly ground
    black pepper

50 g (2 oz) Mozzarella cheese,
    grated

# Meatballs in Sweet and Sour Sauce

This is also delicious made with chicken instead of beef.

✳ *From 1 year*

MAKES 25–30 MEATBALLS

1 onion, finely chopped

vegetable oil

450 g (1 lb) lean minced beef

1 slice of bread made into
breadcrumbs

5 ml (1 tsp) mixed herbs

2 handfuls of parsley, chopped

1 apple, peeled and grated

1 chicken stock cube, crumbled

50 ml (2 fl oz) cold water

SWEET AND SOUR SAUCE

1 onion, finely chopped

1 small green pepper, seeded and
finely chopped

1 x 400 g (14 oz) can of chopped
tomatoes

15 ml (1 tbsp) tomato purée

175 ml (6 fl oz) pineapple juice

7.5 ml (½ tbsp) brown sugar

Sauté the onion in 1 tablespoon of the oil until soft. Mix the onion and all the remaining meatball ingredients together. Using your hands form into 25–30 meatballs and roll in some flour. Sauté in shallow vegetable oil until browned, or, alternatively, bake on a large oiled baking tray (roll in oil first to coat) in an oven preheated to 180°C/350°F/Gas 4 for about 15 minutes. To make the sweet and sour sauce, sauté the onion and pepper in the oil until soft. Add the rest of the ingredients, plus a little freshly ground black pepper, bring to the boil and simmer for 15 minutes. Pour over the meatballs in a casserole, cover and cook in an oven preheated to 180°C/350°F/Gas 4 for 15–20 minutes.

# Peanut Butter Stir-fry

A tasty meal for lovers of peanut butter. Scarlett loves the strips of steak and can't wait to pick them up with her fork so she uses her fingers! This can be served with rice or noodles.

I n a wok or frying pan, sauté the spring onion and carrot strips in the oil for about 2–3 minutes. Add the strips of meat and stir-fry until browned. Mix together the peanut butter, soy sauce and orange juice, add this to the meat and stir-fry until the sauce starts to heat through. Add the courgette strips and beansprouts and stir-fry for about 3 minutes.

**N** ☀ *From 1 year*

MAKES 2–3 PORTIONS

1 spring onion, finely sliced

1 medium carrot (about 50 g/2 oz),
  cut into thin strips

15 ml (1 tbsp) vegetable oil

150 g (5 oz) rump steak, trimmed
  of fat and cut into thin strips

22.5 ml (1½ tbsp) peanut butter

7.5 ml (1½ tsp) soy sauce

the juice of a small orange

1 small courgette, cut into strips

75 g (3 oz) beansprouts

# Colourful Chinese Beef

These thin strips of beef are wonderfully tender and combined with colourful stir-fried vegetables, this dish is ideal for toddlers. If you like, you can mix 75–100 g (3–4 oz) Chinese egg noodles with the strips of beef and vegetables. The saké or sherry will evaporate during cooking, but gives a lovely flavour to the meat.

❋ *From 1 year*

MAKES ABOUT 4 PORTIONS

225 g (8 oz) rump steak

15 ml (1 tbsp) light soy sauce

15 ml (1 tbsp) saké or sherry

1 teaspoon cornflour

30 ml (2 tbsp) vegetable oil

½ small onion, thinly sliced

1 garlic clove, crushed (optional)

75 g (3 oz) broccoli florets

75 g (3 oz) carrot, cut into thin strips

75 g (3 oz) baby sweetcorn, cut into bite-sized pieces

75 g (3 oz) beansprouts

50 ml (2 fl oz) chicken stock (see page 34)

Slice the beef as thinly as possible across the grain and cut into strips. Mix together the soy sauce, saké and cornflour and marinate the beef in this mixture for at least an hour. Heat 1 tablespoon of the oil in a wok or large frying pan and sauté the onion and garlic (if using) for 2–3 minutes. Add the broccoli, carrot and baby sweetcorn, and sprinkle with water. Sauté for about 4 minutes. Remove the vegetables with a slotted spoon. Add the remaining tablespoon of vegetable oil and stir-fry the strips of beef until browned, about 2 minutes.

Return the vegetables to the pan, add the beansprouts and stock, cover and simmer for 2–3 minutes. Serve plain or with noodles or rice.

# Chop Chop

Lamb chops and lamb cutlets are delicious grilled with a few herbs and served with baked potato, or try the variations below.

### Satay Chops
**N** ❋ *From 1 year*

Mix 30 ml (2 tbsp) peanut butter, 2.5 ml (½ tsp) soy sauce, a pinch of mild curry powder, 5 ml (1 tsp) honey and half a finely chopped onion together and simmer for a few minutes. Marinate 2 chops or cutlets for at least 1 hour. Place in an ovenproof dish, cover with foil and bake in an oven pre-heated to 180°C/350°F/Gas 4 for about 50 minutes.

### Chinese Chops
❋ *From 1 year*

Marinate 2 chops in 30 ml (2 tbsp) light soy sauce and 60 ml (4 tbsp) fresh orange juice. Dot with a small knob of margarine and grill under a hot grill for about 15 minutes, turning halfway through.

### Sticky Chops
❋ *From 1 year*

Mix together half a finely chopped onion, 15 ml (1 tbsp) soy sauce, 2.5 ml (½ tsp) red wine vinegar, ½ teaspoon brown sugar and maybe a few drops of Worcestershire sauce. Put 3 lamb chops in an ovenproof dish, coat with the sauce and bake in an oven preheated to 180°C/ 350°F/Gas 4 for about 50 minutes, basting occasionally. If the sauce becomes greasy, pour off the top layer.

# Variations on a Theme of Chilli con Carne

It's surprising, but quite a lot of children enjoy eating fairly spicy food. You can experiment, just adding a little chilli powder to begin with, and gradually adding more as your child gets used to the new taste.

❈ *From 18 months*

MAKES 6 PORTIONS

1 large onion, finely chopped

15 ml (1 tbsp) vegetable oil

450 g (1 lb) lean minced beef

1 small red and 1 green pepper, seeded and diced

30 ml (2 tbsp) tomato purée

1 x 400 g (14 oz) can of tomatoes

10 ml (2 tsp) Worcestershire sauce

400 ml (14 fl oz) good beef stock

2.5 ml (½ tsp) dried oregano

1 bay leaf

a pinch of sugar

2.5–5 ml (½–1 tsp) chilli powder

1 x 430 g (15 oz) can of red kidney beans or 1 x 400 g (14 oz) can of baked beans

Sauté the onion in the oil until softened but not coloured, then add the meat and cook, stirring occasionally, until browned all over. Chop for a few seconds in a food processor and then return to the pan. Add the rest of the ingredients and simmer, covered, for about 35 minutes or until the meat is nice and tender. Remove the bay leaf. This is good served on a bed of brown rice.

*Variation:* substitute a can of baked beans for the kidney beans.

# One-Pot Beef Casserole

Slow-cooked stewing beef has a good flavour and becomes really tender if cooked at a low temperature for a long time. The dish tastes even better the day after it is made.

Sauté the onion, leek and carrot in the oil in a casserole for about 8 minutes or until lightly browned. Add the potatoes and cook for 5 minutes. Remove the vegetables with a slotted spoon and set aside. Add the margarine to the casserole, lightly coat the beef in flour and sauté until browned on all sides. Return the vegetables to the casserole, and add the stock, tomato purée, a few drops of Worcestershire sauce, chopped tomatoes and parsley. Season lightly, cover and cook in an oven preheated to 180°C/350°F/Gas 4 for 20 minutes. Turn the temperature down to 160°C/325°F/Gas 3 and continue to cook, stirring occasionally, for 2½ hours or until the meat is tender. Half an hour before the end, add the button mushrooms.

✳ *From 18 months*

MAKES 6 PORTIONS

1 large onion, sliced

1 leek, trimmed and sliced

275 g (10 oz) carrot sticks

30 ml (2 tbsp) vegetable oil

450 g (1 lb) potatoes, peeled and
    cut into chunks

15 g (½ oz) margarine

450 g (1 lb) lean stewing beef,
    trimmed and cubed

plain flour

900 ml (1½ pints) good beef stock

15 ml (1 tbsp) tomato purée

Worcestershire sauce

1 x 400 g (14 oz) can of chopped
    tomatoes

2 handfuls parsley, chopped

salt and freshly ground black pepper

275 g (10 oz) small button
    mushrooms

# Pasta Passions

When all else fails there's always pasta! In all its wonderful shapes and sizes, it seems to be the one food that is universally popular with children. The skill comes in conjuring up some tasty nutritious sauces and tempting recipes to complement this magic ingredient. An element of disguise may be needed for ultra fussy eaters. When Lara refused to eat meat, I used to sauté a little onion, pepper and minced meat, chop it very finely in a food processor, mix it with her favourite tomato sauce and serve it with spaghetti. She loved it, and it was a gentle introduction to red meat for a child whose stubbornness was not easily overcome.

# Philadelphia Tomato Sauce

Adding cream cheese to a fresh tomato sauce gives it a flavour that children love. Mix with your child's favourite pasta.

Sauté the onion and garlic in the oil until softened. Add the tomatoes, tomato purée, herbs (if using) and a little seasoning to taste, and simmer for 10 minutes. Stir in the cream cheese and Parmesan.

✳ *From 6 months*
MAKES 4 PORTIONS SAUCE

½ onion, chopped

1 clove garlic

7.5 ml (½ tbsp) vegetable oil

4 medium tomatoes, skinned, seeded and chopped

15 ml (1 tbsp) tomato purée

a handful of chopped fresh herbs (basil or oregano) or a pinch of dried herbs (optional)

a little salt and freshly ground black pepper (not before 1 year)

30 ml (2 tbsp) Philadelphia cream cheese or Mascarpone

15–30 ml (1–2 tbsp) Parmesan cheese

# Home-made Tomato Sauce

Tomato sauce with pasta is an all-time favourite with most children. I always make more than I need and store some away in plastic containers in the freezer. It's also good as a sauce for meat or chicken balls or vegetarian rissoles and is an excellent disguise for getting your child to eat his vegetables!

✳ *From 7 months*

MAKES ABOUT 900 ML (1½ pints)

1 onion, chopped

1 garlic clove, crushed

15 ml (1 tbsp) olive oil

30 ml (2 tbsp) tomato purée

2 x 400 g (14 oz) can of chopped
  tomatoes or 1 x 800 g (28 oz)
  can of peeled tomatoes

a handful of fresh parsley,
  chopped

a handful of fresh basil, chopped,
  or 5 ml (1 tsp) dried marjoram or
  oregano

2 g (½ tsp) sugar

a little salt and freshly ground
  black pepper (not before 1 year)

Sauté the onion and garlic (and extra vegetables if using) in the oil until softened. Add the tomato purée and sauté for a couple of minutes. Stir in the chopped tomatoes and the herbs, and simmer, uncovered, until the sauce thickens, about 15 minutes. Season to taste with sugar, salt and pepper.

# Pasta Bows with Three Cheeses

A truly irresistible cheese sauce which provides a good source of calcium for your child. You could cook 65 g (2½ oz) small broccoli florets and add these to the sauce to give it some colour.

Cook the pasta bows in plenty of boiling salted water with a little oil (to prevent the pasta sticking together) for about 10 minutes, or until tender but not too soft. Meanwhile, grate all the cheeses and mix them together. Heat the butter in a saucepan, add the flour and cook for 1 minute. Gradually add the milk, stirring all the time until the sauce is smooth and thickened. Remove from the heat and stir in the three cheeses. Pour the cheese sauce over the cooked pasta and mix thoroughly.

*From 9 months*
MAKES 4 PORTIONS
175 g (6 oz) pasta bows
a little salt
50 g (2 oz) Gruyère cheese
50 g (2 oz) Edam or Gorgonzola cheese
50 g (2 oz) Mozzarella cheese
25 g (1 oz) butter
1 tablespoon plain flour
300 ml (½ pint) milk

# Grandma's Macaroni Cheese

*Despite its bad reputation, many children really do like broccoli. I tested this recipe at teatime on my children and three of their friends, and it was all gobbled up. For this recipe, I like to flavour the milk before making the cheese sauce, but it is not essential.*

❋ *From 9 months*

MAKES 5 PORTIONS

175 g (6 oz) short-cut macaroni

a little salt

a dash of sunflower oil

75 g (3 oz) broccoli, cut into florets

3 tomatoes, sliced

15 g (½ oz) grated Parmesan
   cheese

CHEESE SAUCE

600 ml (1 pint) milk

milk flavouring (piece of onion,
   blade of mace, bay leaf, a few
   peppercorns) (optional)

25 g (1 oz) margarine

2 tablespoons plain flour

5 ml (1 tsp) mustard powder
   (optional)

100 g (4 oz) Gruyère or Cheddar
   cheese, grated

Cook the macaroni in a saucepan of boiling water with a little salt and a dash of oil. Slightly undercook as the pasta will be cooked again in the oven. Meanwhile, steam the broccoli but leave slightly undercooked as well. To prepare the cheese sauce, warm the milk with the onion, mace, bay leaf and peppercorns (if using). Remove from the heat and let stand for about 10 minutes before straining – this will give the sauce a lovely flavour. Melt the margarine, stir in the flour and cook gently. Remove from the heat, and gradually stir the strained milk into the roux to make a smooth sauce. Return the saucepan to the heat, stir in the mustard (if using) and Gruyère or Cheddar cheese and lightly season. Mix the macaroni and broccoli with the cheese sauce and pour this into an ovenproof dish. Arrange the slices of tomato on top and sprinkle over the Parmesan cheese. Bake in an oven preheated to 180°C/350°F/Gas 4 for 20–30 minutes until browned.

# Katie's Broccoli Lasagne

Katie is the cook at Mulberry House School where my five-year-old niece Jacqueline goes. Katie cooks vegetarian meals for the staff and 30 children every day and this is their favourite lunch.

Cook the lasagne in plenty of lightly salted boiling water for 10–12 minutes with the oil to prevent the sheets sticking together. Drain, rinse and separate the lasagne once cooked. Meanwhile, sauté the onion in butter until softened. Add the chopped tomatoes and continue to simmer until they have turned mushy. Whilst the tomatoes are cooking, blanch the broccoli in boiling salted water (not more than 2 minutes as it will be cooked again in the oven). Stir the broccoli florets into the cheese sauce.

To assemble the lasagne, put a thin layer of tomato sauce over the base of a 15 cm (6 inch) square ovenproof dish, and cover with two sheets of the cooked lasagne. Spread half of the cheese and broccoli sauce over the pasta, cover with two more sheets of lasagne, and top with the remaining tomato sauce. Finish off with the last two sheets of the lasagne, the rest of the cheese sauce and sprinkle over the grated cheese. Bake in an oven preheated to 180°C/350°F/Gas 4 for 20 minutes.

❄ *From 1 year*

MAKES 5 PORTIONS

6 sheets lasagne

a little salt

5 ml (1 tsp) vegetable oil

½ small onion, finely chopped

20 g (¾ oz) butter or margarine

3 large beef tomatoes, skinned, seeded and chopped

100 g (4 oz) broccoli, cut into small florets

1 quantity home-made cheese sauce (see page 84)

12 g (½ oz) Cheddar or Gruyère cheese, grated

# Annabel's Vegetarian Lasagne

This is my favourite recipe for lasagne. I prefer traditional lasagne which needs to be cooked in water for a few minutes first. I think it has a much nicer texture than the lasagne which needs no pre-cooking, and the added bonus is that once it's been cooked, you can cut it down to fit the size of your dish.

✳ *From 1 year*

MAKES 6 PORTIONS

6 sheets traditional (or fresh)
  lasagne

a little salt

5 ml (1 tsp) vegetable oil

225 g (8 oz) frozen or 450 g (1 lb)
  fresh spinach

15 g (½ oz) butter or margarine

175 g (6 oz) cottage cheese

1 egg, lightly beaten

30 ml (2 tbsp) double cream

25 g (1 oz) Parmesan or Gruyère
  cheese, grated, plus 1
  tablespoon for the topping

600 ml (1 pint) home-made
  tomato sauce (see page 114)

125 g (4½ oz) Mozzarella cheese,
  grated

Cook the lasagne in plenty of lightly salted boiling water for 10–12 minutes with the oil to prevent the sheets sticking together (or fresh for 2–3 minutes). Run under the cold tap when cooked and separate the sheets. I hang them over the side of a colander. Meanwhile, cook the spinach, drain thoroughly, then sauté in the butter. Blend the spinach together with the cottage cheese, egg, double cream and 25 g (1 oz) Parmesan cheese.

To assemble the lasagne, spread one quarter of the tomato sauce over the base of a 15 cm (6 inch) square ovenproof dish, and lay two sheets of overlapping lasagne on top. Cover with half the spinach mixture, a third of the Mozzarella and one quarter of the tomato sauce. Again lay two sheets of lasagne on top and repeat the layers, using another third of the Mozzarella. Lay two more sheets of lasagne on top and cover with the remaining tomato sauce and sprinkle over the rest of the Mozzarella and Parmesan cheese. Bake in an oven preheated to 180°C/350°F/Gas 4 for about 25 minutes.

# Cheesy Tuna and Pasta Gratin

This is a quick, easy and nutritious recipe to make for your child using store-cupboard ingredients. If you prefer you could use sweetcorn instead of spinach.

Cook the pasta in a large pan of lightly salted water according to the instructions on the packet. Cook the spinach according to the instructions on the packet and then press out any excess liquid and roughly chop the spinach. To make the cheese sauce, melt the butter in a pan and stir in the flour to make a roux. Gradually whisk in the milk. Bring to the boil and cook for about 2 minutes until thickened. Remove from the heat and stir in 65 g (2½ oz of the Cheddar cheese until melted.

Mix together the pasta, cheese sauce, chopped spinach and flaked tuna and season to taste. Preheat the grill. Pour the mixture into a shallow ovenproof dish. Thinly slice the tomatoes and arrange in a single layer over the pasta, season lightly. Sprinkle over the remaining cheese and cook under the grill for about 5 minutes or until golden.

✳ *From 1 year*

MAKES 6 PORTIONS

150 g (5 oz) macaroni or penne

75 g (3 oz) frozen leaf spinach

15 g (½ oz) butter

15 g (½ oz) plain flour

300 ml (½ pint) milk

75 g (3 oz) grated Cheddar cheese

1 x 200 g (7 oz) tin tuna in oil, drained and flaked

2 tomatoes, sliced

# Bow-ties with Chicken and Aubergine

Pasta with tomato sauce is a great favourite with children, and with a little disguise, you can get away with hiding ingredients that your child may not be too keen on eating. The puréed aubergine in the sauce gives a lovely taste, and the little pieces of chicken add some protein.

❋ *From 1 year*
MAKES 4–5 PORTIONS

1 small aubergine, peeled and cut
  into thick slices
a little salt
225g (8 oz) bow-tie pasta
½ small onion, chopped
1 garlic clove, crushed
45 ml (3 tbsp) olive oil
1 x 400 g (14 oz) can of chopped
  tomatoes
15 ml (1 tbsp) tomato purée
a handful of chopped parsley or
  2.5 ml (½ tsp) dried oregano
2 chicken breasts, skinned and cut
  into chunks

Sprinkle the aubergine slices with salt, place in a colander and leave for 30 minutes, then rinse, pat dry and cut into small chunks. Meanwhile, cook the pasta in plenty of boiling salted water for 10 minutes or until tender, and set aside. Sauté the onion and garlic in 30 ml (2 tbsp) of the oil until soft, then add the aubergine and sauté for about 5 minutes. Pour over the chopped tomatoes and stir in the tomato purée and parsley. Season to taste, simmer for 15 minutes and then purée in a blender. Meanwhile sauté the chicken in the remaining oil, about 6–8 minutes, then drain and cut into small pieces. Mix together the chicken and pasta, pour over the aubergine sauce and heat through.

*Variation*: for vegetarians, you could leave out the chicken and mix 100 g (4 oz) grated Mozzarella cheese into the tomato sauce: mix this together with the pasta, sprinkle over a mixture of Mozzarella cheese and freshly grated Parmesan cheese and grill for a few minutes until the topping is golden.

# 10-minute Pasta Primavera

A very appealing pasta dish. You can vary the vegetables according to those your child likes best.

Cook the pasta in plenty of lightly salted boiling water for 5 minutes. After 5 minutes, add the courgette, carrot, broccoli and beans and cook for a further 5 minutes. If using frozen peas, add them 3 minutes before the end. Drain the pasta and vegetables, and stir in the chopped tomato, cream cheese and grated Parmesan. The heat of the pasta should melt the cheeses.

❋ *From 1 year*

MAKES 4 PORTIONS

175 g (6 oz) bow-tie pasta (or penne)

a little salt

50 g (2 oz) courgette, cut into thin strips

50 g (2 oz) carrot, cut into thin strips

50 g (2 oz) broccoli, cut into small florets

50 g (2 oz) green beans, cut in half, or 50 g (2 oz) frozen peas

1 medium tomato, skinned, seeded and chopped

45 ml (3 tbsp) Mascarpone (Italian cream cheese)

3 tablespoons freshly grated Parmesan cheese

# Creamy Tomato and Mushroom Pasta Sauce

Keep some of this sauce in your freezer and you'll be able to rustle up a delicious meal with some freshly cooked pasta in a matter of minutes.

✳ *From 1 year*

MAKES 3 PORTIONS SAUCE

1 small onion, chopped

40 g (1½ oz) butter

175 g (6 oz) brown cap (or button) mushrooms, stalks removed and sliced

2 medium tomatoes, skinned, seeded and chopped

1 tablespoon plain flour

120 ml (4 fl oz) chicken or vegetable stock (see page 34 or 35)

10 ml (1 dsp) tomato purée

30 ml (2 tbsp) soured or double cream

Sauté the onion in 25 g (1 oz) of the butter over a low heat for 5 minutes, then add the mushrooms and continue to cook for about 2–3 minutes. Add the tomato and cook for a further 3–4 minutes. Meanwhile, melt the remaining butter, stir in the flour and cook for about 30 seconds, then add the stock and tomato purée. Cook, stirring, for 3–4 minutes until the sauce is smooth and thickened. Remove from the heat and stir in the soured or double cream. Add this sauce to the mushrooms and tomatoes, heat through and pour over freshly cooked pasta.

# Tempting Recipes with Fresh Fruit

Dessert in my family almost always consists of fruit as there is so much variety now, even in the supermarket. Do give your child fruit that is ripe, and choose fruits that are in season because they will have a better flavour and are often cheaper. Find interesting ways to cut up the fruit or arrange it in a pattern on the plate; little touches like these will go a long way to stimulate your child's appetite!

## Fruity Cone

Buy some large ice-cream cones (you can probably get a better selection from an ice-cream shop than a supermarket) and fill the cones with assorted fruits like strawberries, blueberries, pineapple, tangerines or slices of chopped apple. This encourages your child to eat more fruit and it makes a good portable snack.

## Fruit Fools

Stewed fruits such as gooseberries, rhubarb or apricots make delicious fruit fools. You can either bake the fruits with a little caster sugar in the oven for about 30 minutes or simmer in a saucepan with a little sugar and water. Purée the fruits and mix with Greek yoghurt or a mixture of yoghurt and cream.

## Watermelon Animals

For birthday parties, a spectacular way of serving fruit is to cut a watermelon into the shape of an animal and fill it with an assortment of cut-up fruits.

## Fruity Dip

Mix together equal quantities of cream cheese, fromage frais, Greek yoghurt and fruit purées (dried fruit purées like dried apricots are particularly good). Add a little honey to sweeten if you wish. Serve with chunks of fresh fruit like apples, pineapples and strawberries.

## Summer Berries

When berries are in season you can make a simple but very attractive dessert by spooning some Greek yoghurt mixed with a little honey or a sprinkling of brown sugar on to the centre of a plate and surrounding it with assorted berries.

## Fruit Skewers

Make fruit kebabs from bite-sized pieces of fruit threaded on to bamboo skewers. Use a variety of fresh and dried fruits and unless serving immediately you will need to squeeze a little lemon juice over chunks of banana or apple to prevent them turning brown.

## Fruit Compote

Stewed dried fruits, stewed with a cinnamon stick or vanilla pod perhaps, make delicious desserts, served hot with vanilla ice-cream. You can also add some fresh fruits to the dried fruits but these will need to be stewed for less time.

## Fruit Salad

Unusual fruits are becoming more commonplace nowadays, and to my mind there is nothing nicer than a delicous fruit salad for dessert. I simply cut the fruit into chunks, leaving the skin on where possible as it is a good source of vitamins and fibre and mix with freshly squeezed orange juice. My basic fruit salad consists of 450 ml (¾ pint) freshly squeezed orange juice, 2 oranges, 2 apples, a small bunch of grapes, some fresh pineapple chunks and a banana. To this I add some more unusual or seasonal fruits like papaya, mango, kiwi, peaches, strawberries and raspberries. It's best not to add banana to fruit salad until the last moment as it tends to discolour and turn mushy.

# Real Fruit Ice Lollies

In the summer you can make your own fresh fruit ice lollies. Simply blend fruit juice, milk or yoghurt with fresh fruit, pour into ice lolly moulds and freeze for at least 2 hours. I find that children will eat almost anything if it's frozen on the end of a stick! You can also make two-tone ice lollies by allowing the first layer to freeze before pouring over the second layer. Try some of the delicious combinations below:

✳ *From 9 months*

## Exotic Cocktail MAKES 4.
120 ml (4 fl oz) pineapple juice, 1 peach, equal amount of mango, ½ banana.

## Let's Go Bananas MAKES 4.
Juice of 1 orange, 1 banana and 1 peach.

## Strawberry Smoothie MAKES 4.
120 ml (4 fl oz) milk, 4 strawberries, ½ banana.

## Cider Cooler MAKES 3.
120 ml (4 fl oz) pure apple juice, 1 pear.

## Very Orange Lolly MAKES 3.
120 ml (4 fl oz) fresh orange, clementine or tangerine juice, ½ medium mango (sieve to remove fibres if necessary).

## Fruit Yoghurt Pop MAKES 4.
1 x 150 g (5 oz) pot vanilla yoghurt, 1 ripe banana, 4 strawberries.

## Raspberry Monkey MAKES 3.
1 x 150 g (5 oz) pot of raspberry yoghurt, small banana.

# Baked Apples

These make a wonderful dessert for children: just pop the apple(s) into the oven when you are using the oven to cook a main meal. For young children, remove the skin and mash the flesh of the apple together with the filling.

*From 9 months*
MAKES 2 PORTIONS
1 cooking apple
12 g (½ oz) mixed dried fruit or raisins
60 ml (4 tbsp) water or apple juice
2.5 ml (½ tsp) brown sugar or honey
a knob of butter

Core the apple and score it with a sharp knife round the centre to stop the skin bursting. Stuff with a filling of your choice or leave plain, place on an ovenproof dish and pour the water or apple juice around, trickle over a teaspoon of honey or sprinkle with some brown sugar and dot with a little butter or margarine. Bake in an oven preheated to 190°C/375°F/Gas 5 for about 35 minutes or until the flesh of the apple is soft.

You can stuff the apples with raisins or a mixture of chopped dried fruits like dates, apricots, raisins, currants, sultanas and figs.

*Variation:* for a quick dessert, cook these in a microwave. Simply cover with microwave film, peel back one corner and cook on full power for about 5 minutes.

126

# Fluffy Baked Apple

This recipe uses two different varieties of eating apples instead of the traditional Bramley cooking apple. It's irresistible served hot with ice-cream.

Arrange the apple halves in an ovenproof dish, pour over the apple juice and sprinkle with half the sugar. Bake for 10–15 minutes in an oven preheated to 200°C/400°F/Gas 6 or until the apples are partly cooked. Mix the grated apple with the crème fraîche and cinnamon, divide the mixture among the four apple halves, sprinkle over the remaining sugar and dot with butter. Bake for about 15 minutes longer.

*From 9 months*

MAKES 4 PORTIONS

2 large Golden Delicious apples,
  cut in half crossways and cored

60 ml (4 tbsp) apple juice

8 g (2 tsp) soft brown sugar

1 Granny Smith apple, peeled,
  cored and grated

20 ml (2 dsp) crème fraîche or
  Greek yoghurt

a pinch of ground cinnamon

a knob of butter

# Apple and Summer Fruit Crumble

Hot crumbles bursting with fruit and served with custard
or vanilla ice-cream make perfect comfort food.

*✻ From 9 months*

MAKES 6 PORTIONS

500 g (18 oz) cooking apples,
  peeled and cut into chunks

300 g (10 oz) frozen summer fruits
  (strawberries, rasperries,
  blueberries, cherries)

45 ml (3 tbsp) soft brown sugar

TOPPING

40 g (1½ oz) plain wholemeal
  flour

40 g (1½ oz) plain flour

50 g (2 oz) demerera sugar

a pinch of salt

50 g (2 oz) unsalted butter, cut
  into small pieces

40 g (1½ oz) porridge oats

Mix together the chopped apples and summer fruits together with the soft brown sugar. Put the fruit into an 18 cm (7 inch) square or round ovenproof dish. To make the topping, mix together the flours, sugar and salt and rub in the butter, using your fingers, until the mixture resembles breadcrumbs. Finally stir in the porridge oats.

Cover the fruit with the crumble mixture. Bake in an oven preheated to 180°C/350°F/Gas 4 for about 35 minutes. *Variation*: other fruits which are perfect for crumbles are rhubarb, apple and pear, apple and blackberry, peaches and raspberries, or rhubarb and strawberries.

# Peeping Plums

A really scrumptious cross between a plum tart and a pudding that is easy to make. This is a family favourite in my house.

Sift the flour, baking powder and salt into a bowl and rub the butter into the mixture using your fingers. Mix in the ground almonds and 50 g (2 oz) of the brown sugar. Line and grease a 22.5 cm (9 inch) flan tin and press this mixture onto the base. Arrange the plums cut-side down to cover the base. Sprinkle with 25 g (1 oz) of the sugar and bake in an oven preheated to 190°C/375°F/Gas 5 for 20–25 minutes.

Beat together the egg yolks, sour cream and vanilla essence. When the plums come out of the oven, pour over this mixture and sprinkle the surface with the extra tablespoon of brown sugar. Bake for 20–25 minutes more.

✳ *From 1 year*

MAKES 6 PORTIONS

115 g (4 oz) plain brown flour

pinch of baking powder

pinch of salt

85 g (3 oz) butter, diced

25 g (1 oz) ground almonds

75 g (3 oz) brown sugar plus 1 tablespoon

500 g (1 lb) ripe Victoria plums, cut in half and stoned

2 egg yolks

1 x 142 ml (4½ fl oz) carton sour cream

2.5 ml (½ tsp) pure vanilla essence

# Apple and Almond Pudding

A lovely moist apple pudding which is good served with custard.

*❉ From 1 year*

MAKES 8 PORTIONS

2 cooking apples, peeled, cored
  and cut into bite-sized pieces

18 g (1½ tbsp) soft brown sugar

15 ml (1 tbsp) apple juice

SPONGE

100 g (4 oz) unsalted butter or
  margarine

100 g (4 oz) soft brown sugar

2 eggs, lightly beaten

30 ml (2 tbsp) milk

2.5 ml (½ tsp) almond essence or
  pure vanilla extract

25 g (1 oz) plain flour

75 g (3 oz) ground almonds

5 ml (1 tsp) baking powder

TOPPING

2 eating apples, peeled and cut
  into thin slices

a knob of butter, melted

12 g (1 tbsp) brown sugar

Put the apples, sugar and juice in a heavy-bottomed saucepan. Cover and cook gently until soft but not pulpy, stirring occasionally. Meanwhile, to prepare the sponge, beat the butter or margarine with the sugar until fluffy. Add the lightly beaten eggs (one at a time), followed by the milk and the almond or vanilla essence, being careful not to over-mix. Gradually fold in the flour, ground almonds and baking powder.

Put the cooked apples into a 23 x 18 cm (9 x 7 inch) greased glass ovenproof dish. Pour over the batter and arrange the apple slices for the topping on top. Brush the apple slices with a little melted butter and sprinkle with some brown sugar. Bake in an oven preheated to 180°C/350°F/Gas 4 for 40–45 minutes.

# Eve's Pudding

An old English recipe for a delicious apple pudding, so-called because of the apple given by Eve to tempt Adam.

Beat the butter with the sugar until light and fluffy. Gradually add the egg. Fold in the flour and stir in the milk. Arrange the apple slices in a 28 x 18 cm (11 x 7 inch) greased ovenproof dish and sprinkle over the sugar and water. Spoon the sponge mixture over the fruit and bake in an oven preheated to 180°C/350°F/Gas 4 for 30 minutes or until the apples are soft and the sponge set. Serve hot plain or with custard.

❋ *From 1 year*

MAKES 6 PORTIONS

75 g (3 oz) unsalted butter

75 g (3 oz) sugar

1 egg

100 g (4 oz) self-raising flour

30 ml (2 tbsp) milk

450 g (1 lb) cooking apples, peeled and thinly sliced

40 g (1½ oz) soft brown sugar

30 ml (2 tbsp) water

# Caramelised Apple Flapjack

These make a delicious snack at any time of the day and
will provide an excellent source of energy.

*From 1 year*
MAKES 12 BARS
150 g (5 oz) butter
225 g (8 oz) light brown sugar
3 Cox's apples, peeled and
  chopped
30 ml (2 tbsp) lemon juice
300 g (10 oz) rolled oats
75 g (3 oz) raisins (optional)

Melt the butter in a large saucepan. Add the sugar and heat, stirring occasionally until bubbling. Add the chopped apples. Stir to coat with the caramel and cook over a medium heat for 5 minutes. Stir in the lemon juice and then the rolled oats and the raisins (if using). Line a 17.5 cm (7 inch) shallow cake tin and spoon in the mixture. Flatten with a potato masher and bake in an oven preheated to 200°C/400°F/Gas 6 for about 20 minutes.

Allow to cool in the tin and then turn out onto a wire rack. When cool, cut into about 12 bars.

# Crunchy Apple Sundae

Instead of Harvest Crunch cereal you could use crushed ginger nuts or crushed Amaretto biscuits. You could also use chopped fresh fruits instead of the apple. This is best assembled just before eating.

Put the apple slices in a saucepan together with the sugar and water. Bring to the boil, reduce the heat and simmer for about 5 minutes or until the apple becomes mushy. Set aside to cool. Meanwhile mix the yoghurt with the honey. Into two tall glasses, spoon a layer of apple, followed by a layer of yoghurt and half the cereal and then repeat the three layers again.

*From 1 year*
MAKES 2 PORTIONS

1 large cooking apple, peeled and thinly sliced

15 ml (1 tbsp) soft brown sugar

30 ml (2 tbsp) water

1 x 200 g (7 oz) carton of Greek yoghurt

15 ml (1 tbsp) honey

75 g (3 oz) Quaker's Harvest Crunch cereal

# Berried Treasure

The fruits turn a wonderful rich dark red colour which children love and this is a good recipe for using up fruits that aren't particularly sweet. Don't worry if you don't have all the fruits listed below.

*From 1 year*
MAKES 6 PORTIONS

2 peaches

6 plums or apricots

100 g (4 oz) strawberries

100 g (4 oz) blackberries

100 g (4 oz) blueberries

100 g (4 oz) cherries

40 g (1½ oz) sugar

100 g (4 oz) raspberries

Halve and stone the peaches, and cut each half into four. Halve and stone the plums and apricots and cut each half in two. Put all the fruits except the raspberries into a heavy-bottomed saucepan, sprinkle over the sugar and simmer for 10–12 minutes. Add the raspberries last as they tend to become mushy, and simmer for 2–3 minutes. Serve cold or hot with vanilla ice-cream.

# Simple Summer Fruit Gratin

Crème fraîche is French-style soured cream and I buy it in my local supermarket. However, you could substitute Greek yoghurt or natural fromage frais if you prefer. You can make this using almost any kind of fruit, and it's good hot or cold.

Put the prepared fruit into a glass ovenproof dish. Lay the crushed macaroons or Amaretto biscuits on top and pour over the crème fraîche. Set aside in the fridge for at least an hour. Sprinkle over the brown sugar and place under a preheated grill for a few minutes until golden.
*Variation*: leave out the macaroons and simply sprinkle the top with brown sugar.

*From 1 year*
MAKES 6 PORTIONS
2 peaches, skinned and cut into
    pieces
3 plums, peeled and cut into
    pieces
1 kiwi, peeled and sliced
6 strawberries, sliced
24 g (2 tbsp) raspberries
8 seedless grapes, cut in half
1 banana, peeled and sliced
50 g (2 oz) macaroons or Amaretto
    biscuits, crushed
1 x 250 g (9 oz) carton of crème
    fraîche
18 g (1½ tbsp) brown sugar

CHAPTER FOUR

# Children's Favourites

A selection of favourite recipes with guaranteed 'child appeal'.

# Healthy Fast Food

There's no room for 'empty calories'.

At a very early age, children are exposed to an increasing number of advertisements targeted at them, as consumers in their own right. Young children are easily influenced by TV advertising and packaging. The latest designer children's foods use cartoon characters to promote a wide range of products from canned pasta to sugary fruit juices. Unfortunately the majority of the foods targeted specifically for young children tend to be confectionery, soft drinks, snack foods, sugary breakfast cereals and convenience foods like pizzas and burgers. These heavily promoted foods are affecting the way children eat. There is increasing evidence that they're not just treats, but make up a large proportion of the average child's diet. A recent government report, 'Diets of British School Children', found that fat and sugar intakes were above recommended levels, and that many children's diets were low in nutrients, particularly iron.

There is a common agreement among nutritionists that children get too great a proportion of their energy from fatty, salty and sugary processed foods. The answer is to replace sweet, fatty and salty, savoury foods with nutrient rich foods such as fruit, vegetables, wholegrains, lean meat and fish. However, there is a growing trend among manufacturers to boost the nutrient levels in fatty, salty and savoury products to try to mislead consumers into thinking that these are healthy foods for their children. But do products like highly sugared refined cereals or sweet drinks become healthy just because they contain a few added vitamins?

A high-quality diet is vital for young children. They burn up lots of energy running around during the day, and they also need nutrients for growth and development. They don't have the stomach capacity for large quantities of food, so there's no room for 'empty calories'.

Children have a strong influence on the sort of foods their parents buy. In a recent MORI survey, half the parents of children between 5–11 years old admitted that their children were successful in persuading them to purchase foods they wouldn't otherwise buy! It's especially difficult for parents out shopping with young children when the checkout is laden with sweets perfectly positioned for eager little fingers to reach out and grab. In this country, we munch our way through £1.6 billion worth of crisps and snacks each year and children's favourite foods are more likely to be snacks than main meals as you can see from the result of a recent survey to find the top five children's foods:

1. Crisps
2. Chocolate
3. Ice-cream
4. Biscuits
5. Chips

Lifelong eating habits start early, and a diet high in fat and salt can increase the risk of heart disease and other diet-related illnesses later in life. Too much sugar has led to half the children in this country suffering tooth decay before they are five years old. A recent survey by Gardner Merchant, contract school caterers, found that children in this country spend more than £220 million a year on sweets and snacks on their way to and from school, and seven out of ten children believe their snack-intensive diets are healthy. Are we allowing children too much freedom of choice before they have the ability to make informed decisions?

I hope that this chapter might help you find new ways to wean your little 'junk food junkies' on to Mum's home-cooking by giving suggestions for some children's favourite fast foods using healthy ingredients, thereby giving them what they want but keeping Mum happy too!

# Quick and Easy Pizza

This pizza base is a little like a scone and the great thing is that you don't need to leave it to rise, so it can be ready in just 30 minutes.

Before you prepare the pizza base dough, start sautéing the onion for the topping in the olive oil until softened – this will take about 10 minutes, probably the same time it will take you to make the dough.

To prepare the pizza base, sift together the flours, salt and baking powder. Rub in the butter with your fingers until the mixture resembles breadcrumbs. Whisk together the milk, oil and egg. Make a well in the centre of the dry ingredients and mix in the milk mixture to form a dough. Gradually work the grated Parmesan cheese into the dough. Turn the dough on to a lightly floured board, and roll out into a circle about 25 cm (10 inches) in diameter. Lay this on a large, greased preheated baking sheet. Alternatively, press the dough down into a greased 25 cm (10 inch) flan tin. If you prefer, quarter the dough and roll out to make four individual pizzas.

To prepare the topping, add the tomato purée to the sautéed onion, stir in the oregano and simmer for a few minutes. Spread this over the pizza base and cover with the grated Mozzarella cheese. Arrange the sliced tomato on top, and decorate with a few basil leaves if you like. Sprinkle over the Parmesan cheese and dot with butter. Bake in an oven preheated to 180°C/350°F/Gas 4 for 25–30 minutes.

✳ *From 1 year*

MAKES 1 LARGE PIZZA 25 cm
(10 in) OR 4 INDIVIDUAL PIZZAS

75 g (3 oz) wholemeal flour

75 g (3 oz) plain flour

a pinch of salt

5 ml (1 tsp) baking powder

40 g (1½ oz) unsalted butter

45 ml (3 tbsp) milk

15 ml (1 tbsp) olive oil

1 egg

15 g (½ oz) Parmesan cheese

TOPPING

½ small onion, finely chopped

7.5 ml (½ tbsp) olive oil

45 ml (3 tbsp) tomato purée

2.5 ml (½ tsp) dried oregano

75 g (3 oz) Mozzarella cheese

2 medium tomatoes, sliced

a few fresh basil leaves (optional)

2 tablespoons Parmesan, grated

a knob of butter

# Potato Pizza

These scrummy pizzas have a tasty mashed potato base which is lovely and soft. For fun you can decorate the pizza to look like the face of a clown with cucumber eyes, a cherry tomato nose and a strip of red pepper for the mouth.

❋ *From 1 year*

MAKES 2–4 PORTIONS

450 g (1 lb) potatoes, peeled and
   cut into chunks

25 g (1 oz) butter

1 large spring onion, finely
   chopped, or a handful of
   snipped chives

65 g (2½ oz) plain flour

a little salt and freshly ground
   black pepper

TOPPING

3 medium tomatoes, thinly sliced

70 g (3 oz) Mozzarella cheese,
   sliced

a handful of chopped basil
   or a pinch of dried oregano

25 g (1 oz) Cheddar cheese,
   finely grated

Boil the potatoes until tender, then mash with the butter. Mix in the chopped spring onion and the flour, and season with a little salt and pepper. Using floured hands, shape into two round pizza bases about 13 cm (5 inches) in diameter, and place on a greased or lined (with non-stick baking paper) baking sheet. Bake in an oven preheated to 200°C/400°F/Gas 6 for about 15 minutes or until the edges become a little crispy. Arrange the tomatoes and Mozzarella cheese slices in overlapping circles on top of the pizza. Sprinkle with the basil or oregano and scatter the Cheddar cheese on top. Sizzle under a preheated grill until golden.

# Quick Pizza Toppings

Serving a favourite food like pizza is a great way to get children to eat lots of different foods. Chopping up a selection of steamed vegetables and mixing them into a tomato or cheese sauce makes a delicious topping. It's also fun to lay out bowls with different ingredients and let your child design his own pizza.

B rush the pizza base with olive oil, then cover with a layer of Mozzarella cheese, followed by a layer of the tomato sauce and then sprinkle over the Parmesan cheese and basil (if using). Add any extra toppings that your child particularly likes. Bake as in Quick and Easy Pizza (see page 139).
*Variation*: there are lots of different bases you can buy as a short cut to making a pizza. You can buy ready prepared pizza bases in most supermarkets, or you can use French bread or wholemeal baguettes cut into slices diagonally for mini pizzas or split lengthways for a long pizza plank; muffins or bagels split in half; split pitta bread; or crumpets.

*From 1 year*
1 pizza base
olive oil
65 g (2½ oz) Mozzarella cheese, grated
½ quantity home-made tomato sauce (see page 114)
2 tablespoons Parmesan cheese, grated
a handful of chopped basil (optional)
OPTIONAL EXTRAS
sliced sautéed button mushrooms, sautéed strips of sweet pepper, steamed courgettes, sliced Cheddar and Edam cheese, tomatoes, broccoli, pineapple chunks, peperone, ham, tuna, olives

# Mikey and Mollie Mouse Pizzas

*From 1 year*

MAKES 2 PIZZAS

225 g (8 oz) plain flour or half
    wholemeal and half plain

2.5 ml (½ tsp) salt

10 ml (2 tsp) active dry yeast

4 ml (1 tsp) sugar

olive oil

150 ml (4 fl oz) warm water and
    milk, mixed

1 heaped tablespoon Parmesan
    cheese, grated

some chopped fresh or dried herbs
    like basil, oregano, sage or
    rosemary (optional)

1 quantity Quick Pizza Topping
    (see page 141)

a slice of red pepper, 6 black
    olives, 2 cheese slices and some
    strands of spaghetti for
    decoration

Sift together the flour(s) and salt, then add the yeast and sugar. Gradually mix in 1 tablespoon of the olive oil and the warm water and milk to make the dough. This can be done by hand, in a food mixer using a dough hook or in a processor using a plastic blade. Turn the dough out on to a lightly floured board and knead with your hands for about 5 minutes until it is soft and pliable. Gradually add the Parmesan cheese (and dried herbs if using), and knead until incorporated into the dough. Place the dough in a well oiled bowl, turn to coat with oil (this will help it rise) and cover the bowl with a damp cloth. Set aside in a warm place. Leave to rise until doubled in bulk (about 50 minutes).

Meanwhile prepare the Quick Pizza Topping.

Punch down the dough once it has doubled in size and divide into two. From each ball of dough, roll out one large circle (about 13 cm (5 inches) in diameter) for the face and two small circles for the ears. The base of the pizza should be quite thin. Lay the two large circles on a greased baking sheet and arrange the two smaller circles to form mouse ears. Press the overlapping edges together and brush the surface with olive oil. Cover with the topping, and add some extras too if you like. Bake in an oven preheated to 180°C/350°F/Gas 4 for 20 minutes. Decorate Mikey's or Mollie's face with oval cheese shapes and black olives for eyes, a black olive for the nose, a slice of red pepper for the mouth, and some strands of spaghetti for whiskers.

# Hamburger Heaven

These hamburgers are deliciously moist, and they are particularly good on a barbecue. You can also try making the tomato sauce topping which might help wean your child off the tomato ketchup which tends to be dolloped on so much children's food, so that everything ends up tasting the same. Use a half quantity of the tomato sauce on page 114, then pour into a casserole, over six of these hamburgers. Cover with 75 g (3 oz) Mozzarella cheese sliced, then bake in an oven preheated to 180°C/350°F/Gas 4 for 20 minutes.

Combine together all the hamburger ingredients except for the oil or margarine, form into about 12 small hamburgers and fry in shallow oil until nicely browned and cooked through. Alternatively, dot with a little margarine and grill, turning halfway, until cooked through.

❋ *From 1 year*

MAKES 12 HAMBURGERS

450 g (1 lb) lean minced beef

½ onion, grated

1 Granny Smith apple, peeled and grated

½ chicken stock cube, crumbled

2 tablespoons breadcrumbs

15 ml (1 tbsp) cold water

a little salt and freshly ground black pepper

vegetable oil or margarine

# Beefburger Pie

A simple way to make a really tasty meal using your children's favourite beefburgers or Mum's home-made ones.

❋ *From 1 year*

MAKES 3 PORTIONS

3 frozen beefburgers

1 small onion, finely chopped

1 small red pepper, seeded and
   finely chopped

15 ml (1 tbsp) vegetable oil

70 g (3 oz) brown cap (or button)
   mushrooms, sliced

15 ml (1 tbsp) tomato purée

50 ml (2 fl oz) chicken stock (see
   page 34)

TOPPING

450 g (1 lb) potatoes, peeled and
   cut into chunks

25 g (1 oz) butter

30 ml (2 tbsp) milk

40 g (1½ oz) Cheddar cheese,
   grated

a little salt and freshly ground
   black pepper

Lightly grill the beefburgers and cut into bite-sized pieces. Meanwhile boil the potatoes until tender. Sauté the onion and pepper in the oil for 3–4 minutes, then add the mushrooms and sauté until softened. Mix together the tomato purée and chicken stock and add this to the vegetables, together with the beefburger pieces, and put this into an ovenproof dish (I use a 20 x 15 cm [8 x 6 inch] shallow oval dish).

To make the topping, mash the potatoes together with the butter and milk until creamy. Mix in the grated cheese and season to taste. Bake in an oven preheated to 180°C/350°F/Gas 4 for 20 minutes, and then brown under a preheated grill for a few minutes.

# Baked Bean Volcano

This went down a treat with my three children, and you could use vegetarian sausages for non-meat eaters. Older children will enjoy helping you to assemble this.

Put a pile of mashed potato in the centre of a plate. Make a large hollow in the centre. Run a fork up the outside of the potato. Heat the beans and pour into the hollow. Drizzle a little bean juice down the fork marks. Scatter the grated cheese on top of the beans. Cut up the sausages and place around the potato base.

*From 1 year*

MAKES 1 PORTION

1 portion mashed potato (1 large potato, a knob of butter and 1 tablespoon milk)

1 x 150 g (5 oz) can of baked beans

50 g (2 oz) Cheddar cheese, grated

2 sausages, cooked

# Tuna Melt

A tasty nutritious meal, ready in minutes. I've mixed the tuna with crunchy cucumber but you could also mix it with celery, chopped hard-boiled egg, spring onion, sweetcorn or a combination.

*From 1 year*
MAKES 1 PORTION

1 x 100 g (4 oz) can of tuna in oil, drained

15 g (½ oz) cucumber, peeled and chopped

15 ml (1 tbsp) mayonnaise

1 granary roll or bun, a slice of toast or an English muffin

butter or low-fat spread

1 medium tomato, sliced

1 slice Gruyère, Cheddar or your choice of cheese

a little salt and freshly ground black pepper

Flake the tuna and mix it together with the cucumber and mayonnaise. Cut the granary roll in half, toast it and spread with butter. Pile the tuna mix on top, arrange the tomato slices over the tuna, season lightly and top with the cheese slice. Cook under a preheated grill until the cheese has melted.

# The Good Snack Guide

For many children, snacking on biscuits, chocolates and crisps is a habit and has nothing to do with whether or not they are hungry. In an ideal world, it would be best to restrict our children's food intake to mealtimes. However, sometimes after a long day at school or mid-morning after running around in the garden, children are genuinely hungry and will eat what is available so it's up to us to make a selection of healthy foods readily accessible. For example, it's easy to prepare a bowl of sticks of raw vegetables like carrots, cucumber and celery, and put these together with a tasty dip and some mini portions of cheese in the fridge for a healthy snack any time during the day. It is regular snacking on sugary foods and drinks that does the most damage to children's teeth, so it is important to 'train' young children to enjoy eating healthy snacks like the ones listed below.

## SNACKS YOUR CHILD CAN EAT BETWEEN MEALS

1. Cheese.
2. Savoury biscuits such as rice cakes, crispbread, water biscuits, sesame biscuits, oatcakes.
3. Bread and sandwiches such as pitta bread fingers filled with cream cheese and cucumber.
4. Savoury spreads such as cheese spreads, Marmite, salmon paste, peanut butter **N**.
5. Potato crisps*, corn snacks, Twiglets, home-made popcorn.
6. Vegetables such as carrot, cucumber, celery, tomatoes etc. on their own or with a savoury dip like avocado or cream cheese and chive.
7. Salads such as pasta, tuna and sweetcorn.
8. Fruit such as bananas, oranges, pears, plums, apples, satsumas etc. However, these can cause tooth decay if more than two to three pieces are eaten between each meal.
9. Natural yoghurt sweetened with fresh fruit purée.
10. A bowl of home-made soup or fresh soup from a carton.

*Crisps and corn snacks are all right as part of a balanced diet. Choose a variety made with natural ingredients, and limit your child to three small bags a week. Twiglets are lower in fat and higher in fibre than crisps and similar snacks.

# SNACKS TO AVOID OR LIMIT

1. Sweet biscuits and cakes.
2. Savoury snacks packaged in brightly coloured bags made from puffed corn starch or potato starch, fried and coated with artificial flavourings, flavour enhancers and colouring.
3. Muesli bars and chewy biscuits. All types of sugar, even fruit sugars, are harmful to teeth, and dried fruits are especially bad as they stick to the teeth.
4. Dried fruits such as apricots and raisins: they are fine as part of a meal, but not as an in-between snack.
5. Fruit yoghurts which contain a lot of sugar.
6. Sugary fruit juices and soft drinks.
7. Confectionery: boiled and chewy sweets are particularly bad as they remain in the mouth for a long time.
8. Sugary ice lollies.

It is the frequency with which sweet foods are eaten that does the most damage – try to limit sweet foods to mealtimes. Sweets eaten all in one go will do much less damage than allowing your child to suck a sweet every half an hour.

## TIPS FROM THE TOOTH FAIRY

● Encourage your child to drink water rather than juices or sugary drinks.
● Don't put your child to sleep with a bottle of juice, herbal baby tea or any other sugary drinks. There is less saliva in the mouth at night and saliva acts as a buffer which helps to neutralise acids, thus preventing tooth decay.
● Eating cheese after a meal can reduce the amount of plaque formed on teeth and so reduce the chances of tooth decay caused by bacteria in the plaque digesting sugars to make acid. Cheese helps to neutralise the acids that cause tooth decay so it would be a good idea to get your child into the habit of eating a little piece of cheese at the end of a meal.
● Natural fruit juices are intrinsically acidic and can erode the protective enamel on your child's teeth. When these fruit juices are turned into carbonated fizzy drinks, the effect multiplies.
● Sugar-free soft drinks are no better as they are highly acidic, often containing both citric and phosphoric acids.
● Fluoride is important for building strong teeth that fight bacteria. Fluoride is incorporated into the enamel of the developing teeth that are below your child's gums even before teeth emerge. Children can get fluoride from their drinking water (check the level in your area), or your dentist or paediatrician may prescribe a fluoride supplement.
● If you have an older child who craves sweets, try giving sugar-free chewing gum after a meal. The World Dental Federation has given the sticky stuff its seal of approval. Chewing gum after a meal stimulates saliva, the mouth's natural defence, which helps to neutralise the plaque acids that cause tooth decay.

# Cheesy Animal Cut-outs

These tasty puff pastry animals flavoured with cheese and Marmite can be made either in a single or double layer and are great fun and easy for children to make. Once cooked the cheesy animals can also be frozen with layers of greaseproof paper between them, defrosted and warmed through in an oven preheated at 200°C/400°F/Gas 6 for about 8 minutes. If you don't have animal-shaped cutters then use other shapes like stars or hearts.

*❋ From 9 months*
MAKES ABOUT 8 DOUBLE SHAPES
   OR 16 SINGLE CHEESY ANIMALS
½ x 425 g (15 oz) packet puff
   pastry sheet (thin sheets already
   rolled; there are 2 in the packet
   but just use one) or 250 g (9 oz)
   puff pastry
5 ml (1 tsp) Marmite
50 g (2 oz) grated Cheddar cheese
1 egg, lightly beaten

If using the puff pastry sheet, simply defrost and unroll it. If using ordinary puff pastry, roll out until quite thin on a lightly floured work surface. Cut two of each animal shape from the sheet of puff pastry using a variety of animal shaped cookie cutters. Re-roll the scraps until all the pastry is used up. Working in pairs of animal shapes, spread one side of each shape with a thin layer of Marmite and sprinkle over some of the grated cheese. Brush the underside of the matching pair with egg using a pastry brush. Press this on top of the matching shape making sure the edges are firmly sealed and then brush the top of the pastry with egg.

Place on a lightly greased baking sheet. Cook for about 12 minutes or until golden and puffy in an oven preheated to 200°C/400°F/Gas 6.

If you want to make single layer animal shapes, simply cut out the shapes, spread with a thin layer of Marmite and brush with a little beaten egg. Sprinkle grated Cheddar over each shape and bake in the oven for 10–12 minutes.

# Savoury Bread and Butter Pudding with Cheese and Marmite

Bread and butter pudding has been a popular nursery dessert for many years. By using brown bread with cheese, Marmite, eggs and milk this popular recipe is turned into a delicious wholesome snack or light lunch which is simple to prepare.

Spread the buttered bread with Marmite, trim off the crusts and cut each slice into four triangles. Place four triangles in a small greased ovenproof dish, add half the cheese and put the remaining bread triangles on top. Cover with the rest of the cheese. Beat the egg and milk together, and a little seasoning to taste, and pour this over the top. Bake in an oven preheated to 180°C/350°F/ Gas 4 for 25–30 minutes.

*From 9 months*

MAKES 2 PORTIONS

2 slices brown bread, buttered

Marmite for spreading

50 g (2 oz) Cheddar cheese, grated

1 small egg, lightly beaten

120 ml (4 fl oz) milk

a little salt and freshly ground
   black pepper (not before 1 year)

# Funny Faces

Make faces on a plate, using a selection of raw vegetables and other foods. Below are just some examples of foods you can use. Your child won't be able to resist and will probably give a running commentary – gleefully exclaiming that 'He's bald and only got one eye now!'

*From 9 months*
TO MAKE EYES
sliced hard-boiled egg, cucumber, radishes, round pieces of cheese (like 'Babybel' cheese). Blueberries or raisins are good for making the pupils.

TO MAKE A NOSE
cherry tomato, length of celery, stick of cucumber, carrot, sardine.

TO MAKE A MOUTH
red pepper, row of cooked kidney beans, salami.

TO MAKE THE HAIR
grated carrot, grated cheese, mustard and cress, lettuce, sweetcorn, scrambled egg.

TO MAKE THE CHEEKS
tomatoes, cottage cheese.

# Banana Split

This is simple to make and very healthy to eat. It looks attractive laid out on a plate, especially if you include some more exotic fruits like kiwi and mango. Remember to peel and cut the banana at the last moment or it will turn brown.

Peel the banana and split it in half lengthwise. Lay the two halves on a plate to make a circle with the ends touching one another. Pile the cottage cheese in the centre of the bananas and scatter the chopped fruit on top.

*From 9 months*
MAKES 1 PORTION
1 banana
15 ml (1 tbsp) cottage cheese (or cottage cheese with pineapple)
45 ml (3 tbsp) of a variety of fruits cut into small cubes

# Sandwiches

Sandwiches can come in all shapes and sizes. Try making animal-shaped sandwiches using some fun-shaped biscuit cutters as they're always popular and older children will love giving you a hand. Toasted sandwiches are a meal in themselves, and it is well worth investing in a toasted sandwich-maker which seals and sears the bread.

*From 1 year*
SOME FAVOURITE
SANDWICH FILLINGS:
Peanut butter
Cream cheese or cottage cheese
Egg mayonnaise with salad cress
Cucumber
Marmite
Peanut butter and mashed or
　sliced banana
Mashed sardines
Ham
Grated cheese with tomato and
　lettuce
Cold chicken or turkey with fruit
　chutney

Experiment with lots of different breads – small round pitta bread, slit and stuffed with salad, raisin bread, open sandwiches on bridge rolls, pinwheel sandwiches made with thinly sliced bread, bagels (excellent for a toddler to chew on when he is teething), French bread, pumpernickel bread which is black, or even a sandwich where one side is white and one side is brown. The variations are enormous.

Presentation is very important. A child is more likely to eat something that looks appealing. Sprinkle the sandwiches with salad cress or decorate with thinly serrated vegetables or make your sandwiches into little trains or boats. It doesn't take long and it's fun to do. I think you will find that a lot of toddlers will reach out for your sandwiches and leave behind the sticky buns!

# Toasted Peanut Butter Sandwiches

Spread one of the bread slices with peanut butter and top with a layer of jam. Cover with the second slice of bread. Spread a little butter on both sides of the sandwich and cook in a toasted sandwich-maker which seals the edges, or under a preheated grill (but not too close or it may burn) for about 1 minute. If cooking under a grill, turn over and cook the other side for one minute more. Cut into four triangles.

*Variation*: add sliced bananas to the sandwich before grilling or toasting.

**N** *From 1 year*

MAKES 1 PORTION

2 slices raisin bread or brown
   bread

15 ml (1 tbsp) creamy peanut
   butter

5 ml (1 tsp) low-sugar strawberry
   or raspberry jam

a knob of butter

# Banana-Stripe Sandwiches

A tempting tasty sandwich which is quick and easy to make. Serve immediately or the banana will turn brown.

**N** *From 1 year*
MAKES 1 PORTION
1 slice wholewheat bread
butter or margarine
smooth peanut butter
1 small banana
honey
granola or other crunchy
  breakfast cereal

Spread the bread with butter and then with peanut butter. Arrange two diagonal rows of banana slices on top of the bread and between the rows, drizzle stripes of honey. Sprinkle granola or your child's favourite crunchy cereal on top of the honey. Cut the bread diagonally in half.

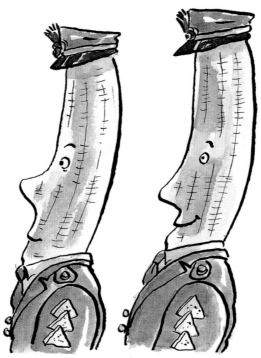

# Sidney the Snake

This is simple to prepare, and a real show-stopper. I buy freshly baked long granary baguettes at my local supermarket which are ideal for this. There are lots of other fillings you could try too, like flaked tuna mixed with grated Cheddar cheese and some cooked sweetcorn or cheese slices with tomato.

With a sharp knife, make 12 cuts in the baguette or French bread, taking care not to cut all the way through to the bottom crust. Leave about 10 cm (4 inches) at one end without cuts to form Sidney's face. Mix the mayonnaise with the chives (if using) and spread every other opening with this mixture. Fold the cheese and turkey slices together and place one in each of the openings that have been spread with mayonnaise. Press the loaf together, wrap in foil and bake in an oven preheated to 180°C/350°F/Gas 4 for 15–20 minutes. Remove the foil once cooked and cut through the openings without the turkey and cheese to make 6 individual sandwiches. Arrange Sidney's body to curl like the shape of a snake and decorate his face. Make a slit for his mouth and give him a piece of lettuce to eat, make two small blobs of mayonnaise for his nose, and secure two cherry tomatoes or radishes with cocktail sticks for his eyes (remove these when serving).

*From 1 year*
MAKES 6 SANDWICHES

1 granary baguette or French bread

50 ml (2 fl oz) mayonnaise

a handful of snipped chives (optional)

6 slices of cooked turkey or ham

6 slices Swiss cheese

lettuce, cherry tomatoes or radishes to decorate

157

# Lettuce Packages

*From 1 year*

MAKES 1 PORTION

grated Cheddar cheese and
  chopped tomato

egg mayonnaise with salad cress

tuna, mayonnaise and sweetcorn

cottage cheese with pineapple or
  chives

chopped chicken with peanut
  butter and grated apple

rice and vegetables

Make stuffed packets of lettuce using large lettuce leaves
and one of the suggested fillings. Why not lay out a
selection of fillings and let your child have fun making the
packages himself.

# Crunchy Celery Canoes

The hollow of a celery stick is just crying out to be stuffed full of goodies. If your child isn't partial to celery, you could use a cucumber or strips of red pepper instead; just cut in half lengthways and make a hollow by removing the seeds.

Wash and trim the celery and cut it into three equal lengths. Stuff with one of the fillings.

*From 18 months*
MAKES 3 PORTIONS
cheese spread or cottage cheese
egg mayonnaise
chicken or tuna salad
cream cheese and a sprinkling of
   raisins
hummus
avocado dip (guacamole)

# Edible Necklaces

Making necklaces using an assortment of non-messy foods is great fun for children, and they're ideal snacks for outings as children can eat them as they go. Use a large needle or, for young children a darning needle which has a blunt end, and choose from the foods listed below to design your own necklace on a length of wool or cord. A good way to encourage your child to eat healthy foods is to thread two or three treats on to the necklace so that your child has to eat his way through the healthy foods before he gets the treats.

*From 3 years*

## HEALTHY FOODS

Miniature cheeses
Chunks of cucumber, carrot, celery or
sweet pepper
Cherry tomatoes
Dried apricots and apple rings
Dates
Breakfast cereals like Cheerios with a hole
in the middle
Round pretzels
Black and white grapes

## TREATS

Licorice Allsorts
Marshmallows
Polos
Wine gums
Biscuits with a hole in the middle
Hula Hoops

# Larder Layabouts

A well-stocked larder is the best form of preventive
medicine known to man.

When buying processed foods, always look carefully at the labels for the list of
contents. There is a legal requirement for food manufacturers to state exactly what
their product is made from. Try to choose foods that are low in sugar, salt and saturated fat,
and which do not contain monosodium glutamate, colouring or artificial flavouring.
Ingredients are always listed in descending order of quantity to make your choice easier.
Remember that saturated fat found in animal products, salt and sugar are the foods to
limit. If sugar or saturated fat appear near the top of the list, think again before buying.
Often labels break carbohydrates into starch and sugars and it is useful to know that 4
grams of sugar make 1 teaspoon. Some individual cartons of fruit juice contain 30 g of
sugar. That represents more than 7 teaspoons of sugar!

Particular care should be taken when choosing commercial baby foods to make sure that
the contents are not bulked out with added water and starches. It's much cheaper and
better for your baby to make your own home-made baby food. It tastes better, it's simple to
make and you know exactly what your baby is eating.

Many processed, prepared frozen products like lasagne or meat pies tend to be high in
animal fat and salt, often contain additives, and are unlikely to be as nutritious as freshly
prepared foods. They never seem to taste as good as the home-made version. When you
have time, it's much better and cheaper to prepare some favourite dishes in bulk, freeze
them in small containers and store for later use.

The next best to fresh are simple frozen foods such as fruit, vegetables, meat and fish
without coatings or pastry. If you are buying fish or chicken in batter or breadcrumbs,
choose larger portion sizes as there will be less coating in proportion to the fish or meat.

Canned fish like sardines, tuna or salmon provide valuable nutrients, and they combine well with lots of different foods. Canned beans like baked beans or kidney beans provide protein, vitamins, minerals and fibre, and make excellent convenience foods. Tomatoes and fruits canned in natural juices are other good stand-bys. Dried peas, beans and lentils are a rich source of protein as are nuts (including peanut butter). Nuts should not be given to young children, however, for fear that they might choke on them. For older children, try some more unusual varieties: my children like sunflower seeds, and they love cracking open and eating monkey nuts (roasted peanuts in the shell). Dried pasta (particularly wholemeal pasta) and brown rice are also good stand-bys in your larder and can provide the basis of many tasty and nutritious meals.

Dried fruits are another good source of nutrients. Let your child try lots of different varieties – I found dried apple, apricots, dates and raisins particularly popular.

## MISLEADING LABELLING

*Sugar-free*
Either no sweetener has been added or the product may have been sweetened with something other than sugar such as honey, glucose, dextrose, maple syrup, molasses or corn syrup (which are just as harmful to your child's teeth), or an artificial sweetener like saccharine (of which the long-term effects are not yet known). Artificial sweeteners are banned from foods for babies and young children. However, young children don't just eat food prepared for babies and young children. From an early age, they eat a range of foods, many of them specifically targeted at youngsters. Look carefully at the ingredients and beware if they contain saccharine, aspartame, sorbitol, mannitol, hydrogenated glucose syrup or acesulfame.

Products which are sweetened with concentrated apple juice or dried fruits are just as capable of rotting teeth as products which contain sucrose. Many of the so-called healthy granola bars which manufacturers claim are bursting with the crunch of wholesome grain goodness are no better than confectionery.

*Fruit Flavour*

Means that the product may have no fruit in it at all. 'Fruit-flavoured' means that some real fruit must have been used, but how much is questionable. Pure fruit juice doesn't need to have a list of ingredients because there is only one ingredient. If there is a list on your child's fruit juice carton and water and sugar are the first two ingredients, you can be sure that it contains very little real fruit juice.

*All Natural*

Be warned that natural ingredients are not always good. Poisonous berries and beetles are natural, but I wouldn't recommend that your children should eat them. Salt, sugar and saturated fat are natural but are not good for a healthy diet. Tartrazine (E102) is a yellow food colour added to many foods which is known to cause adverse reactions in a small minority of children, so manufacturers are replacing this with annatto (E160b), a *natural* yellow food colour extracted from the seeds of a tropical tree. This is sometimes used to colour fish fingers, chicken nuggets or crisps. However, if your child has a history of allergic reactions he/she may well suffer an adverse reaction to annatto, so there is no benefit in its naturalness.

*Vitamin-enriched*

Manufacturers are now adding vitamins to a variety of foods aimed at children, from breakfast cereals and corn snacks to canned pasta and ice lollies. This should not mislead parents into thinking that these sugary, fatty and salty foods are good for their children. Adding vitamins to a poor diet will not transform the diet into a healthy one. The truth is that in turning good natural ingredients into puffed-up sugary cereals, manufacturers are destroying vitamins and nutrients so they are having to add powdered vitamin pills and iron. The once healthy bowl of cereal is looking more like a bowl of sweets.

*Low-fat, Low-sugar*

These claims are only comparative and low-fat spreads, for example, can contain anything from 20–40 per cent fat. Look at the label and choose a spread that contains less than 15 g saturates per 100 g. Many low-fat products, for example some fruit yoghurts, can be full of sugar. A low-sugar product is often simply a lower-sugar variety of a product that contains far too much sugar in the first place. However, low-sugar jams and some low-sugar biscuits like digestive biscuits make a good alternative.

*No Preservatives*

A product may claim to be free of preservatives but salt, vinegar and sugar all have a preservative effect.

*Water and Starches*

These are often used to bulk out small amounts of natural ingredients, so if water or starch appear high up on the list of ingredients, think again. Empty calories may be replacing more nutritious foods. Cornflour, maltodextrin (the gummy stuff used on the back of postage stamps) and potato flour are other types of starch to look out for.

# Top Tips

- Choose baked or boiled potatoes rather than chips. If you do buy frozen chips, microwave and oven chips are lower in fat, and it's best to choose the thick-cut ones as they absorb less fat. Drain the chips on absorbent kitchen paper once cooked. If you want to make proper chips, cut them thick, wash and dry them and fry in oil which is hot but not smoking. Alternatively, blanch in boiling salted water for 3 minutes and drain well. Spread the chips over a well-oiled baking tray and turn them gently so that they are lightly coated with oil. Bake for about 35 minutes, turning occasionally.

- Meat products such as beefburgers and sausages are very fatty, especially the cheaper, economy burgers. Don't give them too often and choose low-fat varieties. Grill rather than fry them and if eating in a bun, choose a wholemeal bun.

- Choose the good old-fashioned breakfast cereals like Weetabix, porridge and muesli, and dress them up with fresh or dried fruits.

- If you are buying fish or chicken in batter or breadcrumbs, choose larger portion sizes as there will be less coating in proportion to the fish or chicken. Fish fingers can contain artificial colours and flavours, and can be made from highly processed minced fish, so read the ingredients.

- Frozen vegetables may well contain more vitamins than fresh vegetables that have been stored for several days as they are frozen within hours of being picked, thereby locking in all the valuable nutrients.

# Caterpillar Salad

Using an ice-cream scoop, I make this salad into the body of a caterpillar. You can make as many scoops as you wish, depending on how many mouths you are feeding. Make the egg, tuna and chicken salad with good bought mayonnaise, maybe adding some chopped vegetables like celery or spring onion, or little cubes of boiled potato.

*From 9 months*

lettuce leaves

egg salad

tuna salad

chicken salad

strips of cucumber, carrot or
  pepper for the legs

cherry tomatoes, stoned olives or
  quail's eggs for the eyes

Make the various salads using egg, tuna or chicken and mixing with ingredients like chopped celery, chopped cooked potato, spring onion, apple or pineapple, mixed with mayonnaise. Lay the lettuce leaves on the plate and scoop the various salads on top, add the finishing touches of the legs and eyes.

# Fish Finger Kebabs

This is a great new way of serving fish fingers, and a novel way to encourage your child to enjoy eating his vegetables. I have chosen three vegetables that are popular with my children, but you could also try chunks of courgette or sweet pepper or even parboiled new potatoes. Remove the fish and vegetables from the skewers for young babies. This is good served with baked beans.

Cut the fish fingers in half. Thread fish fingers, mushrooms, tomato wedges and baby sweetcorn alternately on to four skewers. Brush with melted butter (you could add a little seasoning or herbs to the melted butter if you like), and grill for 10 minutes or until cooked, turning occasionally.

*From 9 months*
MAKES 4 PORTIONS
8 frozen fish fingers
16 button mushrooms, washed
   and stalks removed
4 small tomatoes, cut into
   quarters
8 baby sweetcorn, cut in half
25 g (1 oz) butter, melted

# Sailing Boats

*From 1 year*

MAKES 4 PORTIONS

2 large potatoes, baked

30 ml (2 tbsp) fromage frais or
mayonnaise

1 x 100 g (4 oz) can of tuna or
salmon, drained

2 tomatoes, skinned, seeded and
chopped

a handful of chopped spring onion
or chives (optional)

50 g (2 oz) mixed frozen peas and
sweetcorn, cooked

25 g (1 oz) Cheddar cheese, grated
(to sprinkle on top)

2 slices cheese, cut into triangles,
or 2 corn chips, for the sails

Mash the potato flesh together with the fromage frais or mayonnaise and mix in the flaked fish, tomato, chopped spring onion or chives, and peas and sweetcorn. Pile back into the potato skins, top with grated cheese and bake in an oven preheated to 180°C/350°F/Gas 4 until the topping is golden. Decorate with the cheese or corn-chip sails.

# Sweet Curried Rice with Chicken

Children are often more adventurous with their food than we imagine. I was certainly surprised when I found that my daughter Lara, at the age of one, liked curry. This is a good recipe for using up some leftover chicken or if you have no chicken, just use peas or sweetcorn.

Sauté the onion in the butter, then stir in the curry powder and cook for 1 minute. Add the rice, stir to coat and then cover with the stock and apple juice. Bring to the boil and then simmer for 35–40 minutes. About 5 minutes before the rice has finished cooking, uncover the saucepan and add the peas or sweetcorn. Finally stir in the chopped chicken, and heat through thoroughly.

❋ *From 1 year*

MAKES 3 PORTIONS

1 small onion, finely chopped

15 g (½ oz) butter or margarine

2.5 ml (1 tsp) curry powder

100 g (4 oz) brown rice

450 ml (¾ pint) chicken stock (see page 34)

120 ml (4 fl oz) apple juice

50 g (2 oz) frozen peas or sweetcorn

40 g (1½ oz) cooked chicken, chopped

# Salmon Tagliatelle

A lovely baked pasta dish, which is especially good made with
225 g (8 oz) fresh salmon; this could be cooked in the microwave
or oven (see page 77) and then flaked.

❋ *From 1 year*
MAKES 6 PORTIONS

75 g (6 oz) spinach tagliatelle

3 large tomatoes, skinned, seeded
    and chopped

65 g (2½ oz) butter

2.5 ml (1 tsp) dried oregano

a little salt and freshly ground
    black pepper

1 medium onion, chopped

1 garlic clove, crushed

7.5 ml (½ tbsp) vegetable oil

175 g (6 oz) brown cap (or button)
    mushrooms, sliced

50 g (2 oz) frozen peas

1 x 213 g (7 oz) can of salmon (or
    tuna), drained

25 g (1 oz) plain flour

600 ml (1 pint) milk

100 g (4 oz) Cheddar cheese,
    grated

Cook the pasta according to the directions on the packet, but only to al dente as it will be cooked again in the oven. Meanwhile, sauté the chopped tomatoes in 40 g (1½ oz) of the butter, then sprinkle over the oregano and season to taste. Mix the cooked pasta with this sauce and set aside. Sauté the onion and garlic in the oil until softened, then add the mushrooms and sauté for 2–3 minutes. Add the frozen peas and simmer for 1 minute. Flake the salmon (or tuna), making sure that there are no stray bones.

Melt the remaining butter or margarine in a separate pan, stir in the flour and cook for 1 minute. Remove from the heat and add the milk gradually, stirring all the time to make sure that there are no lumps. Return to the heat, bring to the boil and cook until thickened. Remove from the heat and stir in 75 g (3 oz) of Cheddar cheese, the mushrooms, peas and flaked salmon. Grease a large ovenproof dish or several small dishes, put half the pasta into the dish and spread half the salmon and mushroom sauce on top. Repeat the layers and sprinkle the remaining cheese on top. Bake in an oven preheated to 180°C/350°F/Gas 4 for 25–30 minutes.

# Spanish Omelette with a Tasty Topping

If your child thinks vegetables are 'yucky', how about disguising them in this delicious omelette made with lots of different chopped-up vegetables. You can also cut this into wedges and eat it cold as part of a lunch box or picnic.

Sauté the onion in 15 g (½ oz) of the butter until soft, then add the diced potato and sauté until tender. Add the mushrooms (if using) and continue to cook for 2–3 minutes. In a 20 or 25 cm (8 or 10 inch) frying pan, melt the remaining butter until sizzling. Mix the seasoned eggs with the cooked vegetables, peas and chopped tomato. Pour the egg mixture into the pan, cover and cook over a medium heat until the egg begins to set on the surface. Sprinkle the top with half of the cheese, cover with a layer of tomatoes and sprinkle the rest of the cheese on top. Place under a preheated grill until browned. If your pan has a wooden handle, make sure that it isn't underneath the hot grill – leave it to stick out. Cut into wedges.

*From 1 year*
MAKES 6 PORTIONS

1 small onion, chopped

40 g (1½ oz) butter or margarine

1 medium potato, peeled and diced

50 g (2 oz) mushrooms, sliced
  (optional)

3 eggs, lightly beaten

a little salt and freshly ground
  black pepper

25 g (1 oz) frozen peas

1 medium tomato, skinned, seeded
  and chopped

TOPPING

20 g (¾ oz) Parmesan or cheese of
  your choice, grated

2 tomatoes, skinned and sliced

# Hole in One

This is a fun meal which can be cooked in just a few minutes. Older children will enjoy helping you make this one!

*From 1 year*

MAKES 1 PORTION

1 thick slice white bread

10 g (¼ oz) butter plus an extra knob of butter for frying the egg

1 small egg

a little salt and freshly ground black pepper

Cut a hole in the centre of the bread using the rim of a glass (about 7.5 cm/3 inches in diameter). Sauté the bread in the butter in a small frying pan on one side until golden. Turn the bread over, melt the extra knob of butter in the middle, break the egg into the hole and season lightly. Cook, covered, for about two minutes or until the egg is cooked to your liking. This is good served with baked beans.

# One-bowl Sweetcorn Soufflé

This isn't a proper soufflé, so the timing isn't critical, and it can be prepared in advance. It can also be reheated and eaten the next day.

In a food processor or electric mixer, beat together the eggs, flour, salt and evaporated milk. Melt the butter and pour it into a 15 cm (6 inch) soufflé dish or two smaller round dishes. Stir both the cans of corn and the cheese into the milk mixture and pour this into the dish over the melted butter. Put the soufflé dish in a bain marie (in a slightly larger roasting tin or bowl, half-filled with boiling water), and bake in an oven preheated to 180°C/350°F/Gas 4 for about 40 minutes or until a knife inserted comes out clean.

*From 1 year*
MAKES 5 PORTIONS
2 eggs
1 tablespoon plain flour
a pinch of salt
1 x 170 g (6 oz) can of evaporated milk
15 g (½ oz) butter
1 x 200 g (7 oz) can of creamed sweetcorn
1 x 200 g (7 oz) can of sweetcorn, drained
50 g (2 oz) grated Cheddar cheese

# Creamy Chicken Risotto

Conjure up a quick risotto with a breast of chicken and a can of condensed cream of chicken soup. For a vegetarian risotto, omit the chicken and use a can of condensed mushroom soup.

✳ *From 1 year*
MAKES 5 PORTIONS

25 g (1 oz) butter or margarine

1 small onion, finely chopped

1 small red pepper, seeded and
  diced

1 chicken breast, skinned and
  boned, cut into small pieces

175 g (6 oz) long-grain rice

1 x 295 g (10.4 oz) can of
  condensed cream of chicken
  soup

75 g (3 oz) frozen peas

a little salt and freshly ground
  black pepper

Melt the butter or margarine in a deep frying pan and sauté the onion and pepper until soft. Add the chicken and sauté, stirring regularly, for 3–4 minutes. Add the rice and stir it around in the pan until well coated. Mix in the soup. Fill the soup can with water, add, and simmer, uncovered, for 30 minutes, stirring occasionally. About 5 minutes before the end, add the frozen peas. Season to taste.

# Teatime Treats

It's fun to produce your own home-baked goodies for tea, and they taste so much better than anything you can buy in the shops. All these recipes are simple to prepare and so they are ideal to make with children who enjoy 'helping out in the kitchen' – but remember, you're on your own when it comes to cleaning up!

# Mikey or Mollie Mouse's Favourite Cheesecake

---

❇ *From 1 year*

MAKES 6 PORTIONS

2 x 200 g (7 oz) packets of
  Philadelphia cream cheese

100 g (4 oz) sugar

15 ml (1 tbsp) lemon juice

2.5 ml (½ tsp) pure vanilla extract

2 eggs, separated

BASE

100 g (4 oz) digestive biscuits

100 g (4 oz) gingernut biscuits

40 g (1½ oz) butter, melted

TOPPING

250 ml (8 fl oz) soured cream

24 g (2 tbsp) sugar

5 ml (1 tsp) pure vanilla extract

MICE

1 x 415 g (14¼ oz) can of pears

12 currants for the eyes

6 chocolate chips for the nose

12 sliced almonds for the ears

red licorice for the tails

For the base, crush the biscuits using a rolling pin or a food processor. Stir in the melted butter and press on to the bottom of a 20 cm (8 inch) springform cake tin (I use a potato masher to flatten down the crumbs!). Bake in an oven preheated to 160°C/325°F/Gas 3 for 10 minutes.

For the cheesecake, mix the cream cheese, sugar, lemon juice and vanilla in an electric mixer until well blended. Add the egg yolks one at a time. Beat the egg whites until stiff and fold them into the cream cheese mixture. Pour over the biscuit base and bake in an oven preheated to 150°C/300°F/ Gas 2 for 45 minutes. For the topping, combine the soured cream, sugar and vanilla and carefully spread it over the cheesecake. Bake for 10 minutes longer.

Drain the pears, place around the the top of the cake and decorate with eyes, nose, ears and tails to make six little mice.

# Coconut Kisses

I defy you to eat only one of these! They're definitely one of my favourites, and your children will enjoy helping you make them as well as eat them.

Cream together the butter and sugars. Add the egg and vanilla. Sift together the flour, baking soda and salt and beat this into the mixture. Stir in the chocolate chips, oats and coconut. Form into walnut-sized balls, flatten the top with your hand and place spaced apart on a lightly greased or lined baking tray. Bake in an oven preheated to 180°C/350°F/Gas 4 for 10–15 minutes. The biscuits will harden when they cool down.

✳ *From 1 year*

MAKES 25 BISCUITS

100 g (4 oz) butter

50 g (2 oz) soft brown sugar

50 g (2 oz) caster sugar

1 egg, beaten

2.5 ml (½ tsp) pure vanilla extract

75 g (3 oz) plain flour

2.5 ml (½ tsp) baking soda

2.5 ml (½ tsp) salt

120 g (4½ oz) plain chocolate chips

75 g (3 oz) rolled oats

40 g (1½ oz) desiccated coconut

# White Chocolate Chunk Cookies

These are very easy to make and one of my favourite biscuits. They should be quite soft when they are taken out of the oven so that when they cool down they are crisp on the outside but moist and chewy inside. Leave out the nuts for young children.

✳ *From 1 year*

MAKES 20 COOKIES

100 g (4 oz) unsalted butter

100 g (4 oz) caster sugar

100 g (4 oz) brown sugar

1 egg

5 ml (1 tsp) vanilla essence

175 g (6 oz) plain flour

2.5 ml (½ tsp) baking powder

1.25 ml (¼ tsp) salt

175 g (6 oz) white chocolate
broken into small chunks

75 g (3 oz) pecans or walnuts,
finely chopped (optional)

Beat the butter together with the sugars. With a fork, beat the egg together with the vanilla and add this to the butter mixture. In a bowl, mix together the flour, baking powder and salt. Add this to the butter and egg mixture and blend well. Mix in the chunks of white chocolate and the nuts (if using).

Line several baking sheets with non-stick baking paper. Using your hands, form the dough into walnut-sized balls and arrange on the baking sheets spaced well apart. Bake in an oven preheated to 190°C/375°F/Gas 5 for 10–12 minutes. Allow to cool for a few minutes and then transfer to a wire rack.

# Chocolate Animal Cupcakes

These are fun to make with your children. They are quick and easy and taste delicious even without any icing. Your children will have a lot of fun decorating them to look like different animals. Keep your eyes peeled to make sure the ingredients don't get eaten first!

Beat the butter or margarine with the sugar until light and fluffy. Gradually beat in the eggs. Sieve together the flour, cocoa powder and baking powder and fold this in with the milk. Line a muffin or tartlet tin with about eight paper cases and divide the mixture evenly between them. Bake in an oven preheated to 180°C/350°F/Gas 4 for about 15 minutes, or until a toothpick inserted in the centre comes out clean.

To make the chocolate icing, melt the chocolate and butter together in a microwave or in a saucepan set over simmering water. Remove from the heat and beat in the sugar and water.

Allow the cakes to cool and then ice with chocolate icing and decorate.

✳ *From 1 year*
MAKES 8 CAKES

100 g (4 oz) unsalted butter or
    margarine

100 g (4 oz) caster sugar

2 eggs, beaten

100 g (4 oz) self-raising flour

25 g (1 oz) cocoa powder

5 ml (1 tsp) baking powder

30 ml (2 tbsp) milk

CHOCOLATE ICING

75 g (3 oz) plain chocolate

15 g (½ oz) unsalted butter

50 g (2 oz) icing sugar, sieved

22.5 ml (1½ tbsp) water

DECORATIONS

milk and white chocolate buttons,
redcurrants, red licorice strands,
chocolate chips, chocolate buttons
and a packet of dolly mixtures

# Apricot and Coconut Muffins

Everyone in the family will love these delicious moist muffins. Serve plain or, for a special occasion, warm some apricot jam with a little water, brush this over the tops of the muffins, sprinkle over a little desiccated coconut and stick a glacé cherry on top.

✳ *From 1 year*

MAKES 10 MUFFINS

2 eggs, lightly beaten

120 ml (4 fl oz) vegetable oil

1 x 120 ml (4 fl oz) can crushed
  pineapple in natural juice

50 g (2 oz) dried apricots, finely
  chopped

75 g (3 oz) caster sugar

25 g (1 oz) desiccated coconut

100 g (4 oz) plain flour

7.5 ml (½ tbsp) baking powder

a pinch of baking soda

a pinch of baking salt

In a large bowl, mix together the first six ingredients. Sift together the flour, baking powder, baking soda and salt and fold these into the first mixture (do not over-mix). Line a muffin tray with paper cases, pour in the batter and bake in an oven preheated to 180°C/350°F/Gas 4 for 25–30 minutes.

# That Takes the Biscuit

These scrummy no-bake chocolate squares are perfect to make with young children for a special tea party.

Break the chocolate into squares and put it into a glass bowl together with the butter, syrup and cream. Place the bowl over a pan of simmering water and stir until melted. Alternatively use a microwave and cook on High for about 3 minutes, stirring halfway through. Roughly break up the biscuits – your children will enjoy doing this! In a bowl, combine the broken biscuits with the almonds, raisins and chopped cherries. Pour over the melted chocolate and mix thoroughly. Spoon the mixture into an 18 or 20 cm (7 or 8 inch) square tin, lined with foil, and press down firmly (a potato masher will do the trick). Leave in the fridge to set. Cut into small squares.

**N** *From 18 months*
MAKES 16 SQUARES
115 g (4½ oz) plain chocolate
100 g (4 oz) unsalted butter
30 ml (2 tbsp) golden syrup
30 ml (2 tbsp) double cream
200 g (7 oz) digestive biscuits
50 g (2 oz) flaked almonds
40 g (1½ oz) raisins
50 g (2 oz) glacé cherries,
  chopped

CHAPTER FIVE

# Special Needs

As well as being the fuel for our bodies, food can cause problems like allergic reactions, diarrhoea and excess weight. But how do we cope when things go wrong?

# Overweight Children

In this country, 10 per cent of boys and 13 per cent of girls are overweight by the age of eleven and children as young as three have been known to have fatty streaks in their arteries from eating too much fat.

Obesity does tend to run in families, so if you or your husband have a tendency to be overweight, make sure that your child gets the nutrients he needs without eating too much fat. Once children get to a certain age, it becomes more difficult to lose the weight they have put on, so it is important to control your child's diet early if they are becoming seriously overweight. Whereas there is little relationship between the weight of a child under the age of five and the weight he will be in adulthood, statistics show that over the age of five, there is an increasing link between adult weight and childhood weight.

The Traffic Light Diet is a simple guide to choosing the right foods. Young children need plenty of nourishment, so unless your child is seriously overweight, in which case you should seek professional help, don't take drastic measures. Your aim should be to keep your child's weight steady and as he grows, he will slim down.

Try to cut out processed and fatty foods and between-meal snacks like crisps and biscuits. Beware of hidden calories in foods like canned fruit in syrup, sausages and soft drinks. Encourage your child to eat plenty of fruit and vegetables – unusual fruits make delicious treats instead of sweets and chocolates. Serve water instead of sugary drinks. If your child is used to eating large quantities of food, try to develop interests, particularly physical activities, to help take his mind off food. It helps to serve meals on smaller plates and encourage your child to spend longer over his meal rather than gulp it down.

It may not be feasible to ban sweets entirely, particularly if your child comes into contact with other children who eat sweets and crisps etc. Limit your child to when and how much can be eaten. Don't worry if your child binges at birthday parties and when he eats out – it's his overall diet that is important. If you are worried about your child being overweight, follow the simple diet overleaf and set your child into a healthy eating pattern.

# The Traffic Light Diet

## STOP

HIGH ENERGY – LOW NUTRIENTS

These foods are not needed for health and should be eaten only very occasionally.

*The sweet foods*

- sugar (white, brown, raw, icing), glucose, treacle, molasses, syrups, condensed milk, honey, jam, marmalade
- jelly, ice lollies, ice-cream toppings, canned fruit in syrup, fizzy drinks, squash, fruit juice with added sugar
- flavoured and sugar-coated cereals
- fancy cakes, iced or chocolate biscuits, sweets, chocolate

*The high-fat foods*

- lard, dripping, oil, cream, butter, margarine, pastry, pies
- all fried food, roast vegetables, chips, crisps, fatty meats such as sausages, salami and beefburgers and many convenience foods.

## SLOW

HIGH ENERGY – HIGH NUTRIENTS

These foods are good for you and some are needed every day but too much can put on extra weight.

Choose from each group and eat in moderate amounts:

- meat, fish, shellfish, poultry
- eggs, cheese, milk, yoghurt, beans and lentils, baked beans, peanut butter
- bread, water biscuits, crispbreads, plain biscuits (occasionally), breakfast cereals, porridge oats, potatoes, rice, pasta.

## GO!

LOW ENERGY – HIGH NUTRIENTS

Eat plenty of

- fruit and vegetables.

They are full of vitamins, minerals and fibre. Don't have more than 250 ml (8 fl oz) fruit juice per day as it is quite high in calories.

Take regular exercise.

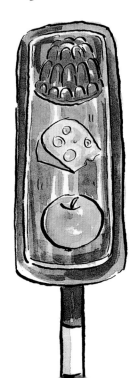

# Food Allergy

Allergies to food are not very common and unless there is a history of allergy in the family, it is not something you should be unduly worried about. Unfortunately the term 'food allergy' is often used incorrectly to describe food intolerance which is generally short-lived and not the same as a true food allergy which involves the immune system.

Food allergy probably exists transiently in up to 5 per cent of children in their first years of life. I say transiently because 90 per cent of food allergies have disappeared by the age of five. Certainly 80 per cent of children who could not tolerate cow's milk in the early years, are able to drink milk by the age of three.

Foods most likely to cause an allergy are cow's milk and dairy products, eggs, fish (particularly shellfish), and nuts. For ease of reference, any recipe containing nuts in this book has been labelled with an **N**. Citrus fruits, wheat and, occasionally, artificial food colourings and additives can also induce an allergic reaction. With the exception of whole nuts, there is no reason why any of these foods should not be given from 6 months (but remember that cow's milk should not be given as a drink before one year). If, however, one or both parents suffer from an allergy to any of these foods then delay the introduction of the offending food or food group, and seek a doctor's advice before giving it to your child. If it is a basic food like milk, you will need to consult an expert who will design a special diet for your child.

If you think that your child is suffering from a food allergy, consult your doctor.

# Food and drink for sick children

If your child is unwell and off her food, drinks are important, so try offering nourishing drinks like milk or milkshakes. Soups are good too, particularly a lovely home-made chicken soup. Otherwise try soft foods like scrambled egg, steamed fish or mashed banana. Healthy eating may have to be forgotten for a few days, but try not to let this drag on. After a long period of poor eating it might be a good idea to try one or two weeks of a multi-vitamin and iron supplement.

If your child is on antibiotics, then it is a good idea to give her live yoghurt. This is available in fruit flavours, or sweeten natural live yoghurt with a little honey or fruit purée. Antibiotics kill off both bad and good bacteria in the intestine and eating live yoghurt helps to restore the balance.

## VOMITING AND DIARRHOEA

If a child is suffering from vomiting and diarrhoea, stop feeding him solids and milk (the bowel needs to rest for the child to get well again), and just give plenty of Dioralyte, a salt and glucose compound available at chemists which you make up with water. Give this until the vomiting or diarrhoea has stopped. Plain water or fruit juice is not adequate for more than 4–6 hours as your child will get excessive loss of salts from the body if not replaced. The most important thing is to make sure that your child does not get dehydrated. Excessive dehydration can be very serious for a small child, and vomiting is potentially more serious than diarrhoea as it is more likely to lead to dehydration. Encourage your child to drink and if he is drinking and passing urine, he should be a lot better within 24 hours and be ready to eat some light food. If your baby is under 1 year and has diarrhoea or has been vomiting for more than 6 hours, you should seek medical advice.

If your child is suffering from diarrhoea only, stop milk and solids for one meal only, then re-introduce light food if your child feels hungry. Breast milk is fine as it contains anti-diarrhoeal and anti-infectious properties. You can use plain water or diluted fruit juice only for up to 24 hours for children over the age of one, but it's better to use Dioralyte. If the diarrhoea persists for more than 24 hours, then you should seek the advice of a doctor.

STOP : solid food and milk (except breast milk)
GIVE : glucose drinks like Dioralyte

*After 24 hours*
STOP : milk, fruit, vegetables and meat until the following day
GIVE : glucose drinks like Dioralyte, rice, yoghurt, tapioca or semolina, grilled fish, bread, cereal or plain biscuits

## CONSTIPATION

If your child is constipated, it is important that he has plenty to drink. He will need at least 6 cups a day (6 x 250 ml/8 fl oz). Decrease sugary drinks and encourage him to drink water. Give foods which are good sources of fibre – something simple like baked beans on wholemeal toast or high-fibre breakfast cereals which can be eaten at any time during the day (see the list below for other good sources of fibre). If necessary, your doctor will prescribe a mild laxative suitable for young children, but it should be enough to include plenty of fibre and unprocessed foods in your child's diet.

STOP : highly processed foods like cakes and sweets, and stodgy food like rice pudding and macaroni cheese
GIVE : fruit and vegetables, stewed prunes, dried fruit compote, fruit juices (prune juice is particularly good), bran and wholegrain cereals like All Bran, Weetabix or Raisin Bran, wholemeal bread or added fibre white bread, pulses (lentils, beans and peas, which can be added to soups and stews).

# Index

# ACKNOWLEDGEMENTS

I am indebted to the following people for their help in the preparation of this book:
Dr Margaret Lawson, Fiona MacIntyre, Joanna Carreras, David Karmel,
Evelyn Etkind, Susan Fleming, Martin Lovelock, Dr Stanley Rom, Dr Tim Lobstein,
Susan Tanner, Christine Carter, Hamid, Letty and Marina, Beryl Lewsey, Fiona Lewis
and in particular my husband Simon Karmel who has stoically eaten his way
through all the recipes in this book.

# Also by Annabel Karmel

*Annabel Karmel's New
Complete Baby and
Toddler Meal Planner*
0 09 188088 2

*Annabel Karmel's
Small Helpings*
0 09 186373 2

*Annabel Karmel's
Complete Party Planner*
0 09 187526 9

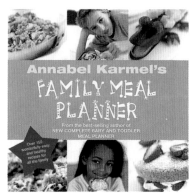

*Annabel Karmel's Family
Meal Planner*
0 09 186795 9

*Annabel Karmel's SuperFoods for
Babies and Children*
0 09 187902 7

All are published by Ebury Press and are available from good bookshops
Alternatively, call TBS Direct on 01206 255 800